# How to Succeed at High School

By Dillon Valderemao

How to Succeed at High School

© 2017 Dillon Valderemao

## About the Author

I have been a teacher for more than 20 years. I graduated as an English and History teacher in the early 90s and have taught a variety of subjects in schools across Australia, New Zealand, the UK, and the South Pacific. During the last decade, I was the Head of a Secondary School in Melbourne, Australia.

I enjoy reading, writing and working creatively, walking, gaming on my Xbox or PC and spending time with my family. I currently live in Melbourne with my wife, two sons and many pets.

I would love to hear from readers. If you have suggestions, feedback, comments or would just like to share your story send an email to dillon@howtosucceedathighschool.com and I will endeavour to get back to you.

## Acknowledgements

This book would not have been possible without the assistance and support of many people. My wonderful wife, Amanda, has supported me from the beginning. Her tolerance of the lonely hours I spent tapping away in the office is beyond measure. My awesome family (Mum and Sis) have believed in me even when I didn't. Despite the years of zero productivity they were always confident that I would make it. My good friend Donna, is not only a fellow Sci-Fi fan but provided valuable feedback and advice on the manuscript. And finally, the staff and students of Gilson College, who, even though they may not be aware of it, are indirectly responsible for much of the information in this book. Thank you all and may this book bless you just as you have blessed me.

## Dedication

I've written this book for my two sons, Elias Tennyson Valderemao and Emmanuel Keats Valderemao; and for my 'other son' Jourdain Connor Moore. I hope this brings you success now and in the future.

# Table of Contents

# Introduction

I have taught or been involved in high school for more than 20 years, in a variety of different countries, and in all that time I have worked with thousands of students, their parents and teachers, and have seen what does and what does not work in high school. I have collected a lot of information about learning, study and succeeding at school and have attempted to distil that information into this easy-to-read book.

Over the years, I have come to learn that success in high school is not about how smart you are – let me repeat that – success in high school is NOT about how smart you are. It's about having the right attitude, being organised and planning to succeed. You see, those people that succeed don't do it accidentally – they think about it, they plan for it and they work towards it in a logical fashion. And that's something that you can learn!

Of course, there are students who are 'gifted', have a high IQ and always seem to do everything right. They live in the "zone"! What these people don't realise is that the 'zone' moves as time passes and what is 'great' now will only be 'ordinary' in a few years' time. When that happens, the 'gifted' people, who have relied on their gifts, will suddenly be out of their depth and not so gifted any more.

If you truly want to be successful at high school – and beyond– you need to learn HOW to be successful: What are the keys to success? What is the recipe to good grades? What are the co-ordinates to an exciting and fulfilling high school career?

Grab a pen, find a nice comfortable chair, and prepare to change your life!

## About this Book

This book can be read through from cover to cover or the most relevant items read before other, less relevant parts. There may even be parts of the book that are not relevant to you at all – you don't even need to read them to benefit from the book. Any ideas that you pick up from reading this book will help you become more successful at high school, and the more that you adopt, the more successful you will be.

Throughout the book, opportunity has been provided for your own notes, ideas, goals and thoughts and I encourage you to jot down anything that comes to mind. If you read this book in a proactive way – with an aim to 'do' and 'learn' and 'change' – you will benefit much more from it than if you just read it like you would read a novel.

As you complete reading a section stop and think about what you've just read. How does it apply to you? How can you use the information to improve your opportunities for success? Contemplate the implications of what you have learned and consider what actions you will take. Write them down if you can. Only when you've absorbed the information should you keep reading.

I recommend that you keep a pad of paper and a pen handy as you read this book. As ideas or actions come to you jot them down so that you don't forget them. Use these ideas to cement your understanding.

Action steps have been provided in many sections – something to do that is relevant to what was just read. It is a good idea to complete these actions as soon as you read the relevant section because they will clarify the ideas in your mind and prompt you to immediate action.

At the end of each part there is an opportunity to think about how you will put what you have learned into action. This Action Plan should be implemented as soon as possible because if you wait – even a few days – the good idea will soon get lost in the busy schedule of your life and nothing will change.

Resources have been included at the end of the book, such as documents or templates, which are there to make working towards your success much easier.

Finally, don't read this book only once and then put it away. There are so many useful ideas in this book that you will not absorb them all in just one reading. If you read this book only once you will miss much of what it has to say and its impact on your success will be diminished. Instead, read it every few months, or a couple of times each year – you will find that on the second reading you will reinforce ideas that you picked up earlier and notice ideas that you missed the first time. The more times you read it the more this book will help you.

# A Note for Parents (make sure your parents read this!)

Ultimately your child is responsible for their own learning, but that doesn't mean you cannot assist them as much as possible. Multiple studies have demonstrated that when parents are involved in their child's learning that child is ahead of peers with results and better able to handle the challenges of school. My experience shows that this support is usually quite effective when the child is in primary/elementary school but diminishes when the child enters high school. It shouldn't be this way!

Your child needs parental support throughout the educational process. The learning doesn't stop at the beginning of high school, in fact, it becomes more complex. Not only that, but the environment of high school becomes more challenging and when the hormones start developing, learning can take a back seat. Parental support is vital during this time.

For boys, it is particularly important that dads become involved and take an interest. A reading father is one of the most valuable things a young boy can see.

So how do you help your child become a success at high school?

- Communicate with your child on a regular basis – not only when things are going wrong. Ask them often how their day was, what did they learn, what challenges have they faced, etc. Ensure these are casual friendly questions, not forced interrogations.
- Communicate with your child's teachers often. Start at the beginning of the academic year by

introducing yourself and asking what you can do to help them (teachers love this and it will make all future conversations easier!) – and then do what they suggest.

- Take an interest in your child's work. "You're learning about volcanos, tell me about them", "you're studying Macbeth – the local theatre company is presenting that – do you want to go next week?" "you got a part in the play, well done! Can I help you rehearse?"

- Do not do the work for them! You need to be helping your child learn and we learn by doing and by making mistakes. If you do their work for them you are not helping them!

- Have a common study area like the dining room table where everyone does their homework. Do not allow bedrooms to become private study areas because bedrooms should be reserved for rest and relaxation – not work – and despite the best intentions private study areas provide too many distractions.

- Have a study timetable kept in a visible place – like on the fridge. Let them make it (this is discussed later in the book) but help them keep accountable to it.

- Read this book. The information here is targeted at your child but it is also important that you know about the strategies of success. When you are familiar with these principles you will be able to more effectively support your child – you may also learn something that you can apply to your own life.
- Don't force! Being forced to do something doesn't change thoughts, habits or attitudes. The positive suggestions in this book should be followed but ensure that your child sees the benefits and **chooses** to make the changes. The decision must be theirs, not yours.
- Finally, try to 'balance' the pressure – by this I mean don't constantly hound them to succeed, but also don't let them make excuses and avoid study altogether. Avoid the extremes and instead be a guide, a mentor and a support for your child.

## A Note about Evidence

Much of the information in this book is based upon years of experience working with students, parents and teachers, and doing lots of reading. Many of the principles, ideas and practices that are discussed are based upon sound scientific research carried out by many different professionals over the past decades around the world. Much of it is now a part of the research 'canon' – meaning that is it known by many people who have not studied the original research. For the sake of simplicity, I do not reference any research papers or studies in this book, but if there is something that interests you a search on the Internet will provide a lot of information on a chosen topic.

## A Note about Success

This book is obviously about success, but what exactly is 'success'? Success is like taste – it's different for everyone! One person loves pomegranate juice, another person hates it. It's not the juice that's different, it's their taste. So, too, with success. What one person sees as successful, another doesn't, and what one person strives for with daily hard work, another doesn't even notice!

This book is about success in high school – that means completing high school with high grades – however they are measured in your part of the world. But that doesn't mean that if you don't finish high school you are a failure, or that if you do get high grades at the end of high school you will be successful in life. Unfortunately, high school and life are not that closely related. I've taught students who have achieved top grades in their class but are now unemployed. I've also taught students who didn't achieve much at high school who are now earning big money in industry.

For the purpose of this book when we talk about success we mean high grades at the end of high school, but the skills, processes and procedures you will develop on this journey will give you a better chance of success AFTER high school. So, don't get distracted by the words SUCCESS or FAILURE – they are just words and their meanings are very subjective – they mean different things for different people. You must define your own success!

## A Note about Age Level

This book is written for students who are just starting out in high school – in most places that's about 12 years old. The advice is directed at students who are this age but many of the ideas (and words used) are more advanced than you would expect for 12 year olds. This has been done on purpose for a few reasons:

- Firstly, students who are interested in success should want to be ahead of their peers – if not, they would probably not be interested in success;

- Secondly, students who are interested in success need to be doing more than what people expect – if you do what people expect you will usually be average;
- Thirdly, stretching your mind is important – use this opportunity to think about new ideas and learn new words. If you encounter an idea or concept for the first time think about it, discuss it with friends who also want to be successful. If you find a word you do not know look it up and familiarise yourself with it. Read it again in context so that you understand its meaning. If you don't understand an idea or word ask a parent or teacher to explain it. If you don't, you will miss an opportunity to improve yourself.

If you are not 12 years old it doesn't matter. The information in this book can be used by students who are older or younger – the only prerequisite is that you want to be successful!

# Part 1 – Attitude

*Your attitude, not your aptitude, will determine your altitude.*

Zig Ziglar

Your attitude plays a huge part in how successful you will be – basically, those students who are positive will succeed and those who are negative will not. I've seen this in school repeatedly. I've known students who seem to have many advantages (they are smart, work hard, come from a stable home, etc.) fail because they are always negative about their own abilities and chances of success. Conversely, I've known of students who seem to have much less going for them (struggle at school, come from a troubled home, face many challenges, etc.) who succeed because they are confident and are driven to achieve.

Of course, there is more to it than just attitude. A student who has a positive attitude but doesn't do any work is not going to succeed, but attitude is a big part of the equation. In fact, attitude is the foundation of success. You cannot succeed without the right attitude, and you cannot remain successful without it.

That's why this book about success in high school is starting with attitude – if you get that right the rest should be easier. So, let's look at how your attitude can make a difference.

## Self-Confidence

Self-confidence is believing in yourself – believing that you can achieve something. It may be something in particular – like climbing a tree or passing a test, or it may be a more general belief in your ability to achieve in lots of different areas. Someone who is self-confident 'knows' that they can do it – even if they've never tried it before. They may not be able to do it – at first – but they are confident, will keep trying and will eventually succeed. Without that confidence, they wouldn't have tried in the first place.

Having confidence doesn't mean you believe unbelievable things – like being able to fly or learn a new language in ten minutes – it means that you have done the work and believe that you can achieve – even if others don't think you can. It also means that you will not be stopped by obstacles – if something gets in the way you overcome it, because you know you can.

Self-confidence is a personal thing – no one else can give it to you or take it from you. It's a state of mind which leads you towards success and in many cases it will not be shared by others – especially in high school. There will be many times when your peers (and even your friends) will not believe in you – will not believe that you can do it. Sometimes they may be right but that doesn't mean that they will always be right. You should not be led by the crowd or accept the crowd's beliefs.

Remember, high school is not life – your life will really begin AFTER high school, so don't let the beliefs of others set you on a path that is less than success for you. Be confident in yourself and your abilities and you will eventually succeed.

- *ACTION – when you have a few minutes alone stand in front of the mirror and look at yourself. YOU should be your biggest fan, the one who believes in you more than anyone else. Tell yourself that – in a loud, confident voice say "I believe in you. You can be successful." Do this at least once each day.*

## Visualisation
Something that can help you be more confident is visualisation. Visualisation is a term to describe making up 'movies' of life in your head and replaying them to yourself. It is a practise that is common amongst

successful people and will help you to be more successful. Visualisation helps you to mentally prepare for a situation so that your mindset is right – it will help you develop confidence and the right attitude.

Let's look at an example: say I have an important presentation in class tomorrow. Once I've prepared the presentation (no, visualisation will not do the work for you!) I create a movie of myself successfully presenting to the class. In my visualisation, I will be confident and eloquent, the teacher and all the other students will enjoy the presentation and it will be a great day. I will then spend some time replaying the movie in my head. A place where there are no distractions (bed, the shower, a walk, etc.) is the best place for visualising.

Make sure your visualisation is realistic (visualising the Principal jumping through a window wearing a clown suit may be fun but it won't be helpful) and positive (if you visualise yourself failing there is a higher chance that you will). A positive visualisation will build your confidence – even though, in reality, you haven't done anything yet – and make it more likely that you will be successful. The power of visualisations is that your subconscious mind cannot tell the difference between real life and what you visualise. If you visualise something positive those positive feelings will be real for your mind and will reinforce the positive outcome when you are actually doing the action.

Visualisations can cover literally anything – school work, interactions with other people, physical activity, etc. If you visualise yourself successfully completing an action before you actually complete it your confidence will grow and there's a better chance that you will be more successful at it.

- *ACTION – Choose an activity that you are planning to complete at school – it can be physical (shooting a basket), academic (presenting a research assignment), or relational (a potentially difficult interaction) – and create a visualisation of you completing the activity successfully. Replay it multiple times. Those positive feelings you are enjoying are REAL to your brain. Keeping visualising and see what impact it has had on the actual activity. It may not have gone like you visualised but did you approach it more confidently? Are you less intimidated by it next time? Keep practising and it will get better.*

# Sharing Problems

An important key to success is that you shouldn't to do it alone. Many people believe that they must deal with their problems in isolation – that if they ask for help they are somehow weak and stupid. Nothing could be further from the truth! The most successful people in this world are surrounded by people who support them and assist them to be the best they can be. The stupid people are the ones stuck in the distance trying to solve all their own problems.

Let's face it, for someone in high school problems are everywhere! Problems with your classwork, with other students, with teachers, with parents or personal problems – there is no end to problems. That's why it's important to share your problems with others – don't try to deal with them alone. Following are some suggestions for sharing your problems. Some of them may not work for you but keep trying until you find ones that do.

### Sharing with Friends

Your friendship group is a valuable source of support while you are in high school – and beyond. Your friends usually know things about you and you can trust them (I would suggest that if you can't trust them they are not friends!). Sharing your problems is usually an automatic part of friendship so use your friends to 'offload' some of your issues. If the problem is at school your friends are may be going through the same thing and you can discuss it together. Just talking about it will make you feel better and may also help.

If the problems are schoolwork-related it may be an idea to develop a study group of friends or other classmates who are also interested in success at high school. Meeting at lunch time to discuss an assignment or study for a test is a constructive way to approach the problem, it will probably help you develop new friendships, and will lead towards success in that class.

- *ACTION – talk to your friends to learn which of them would be interested in meeting regularly (maybe at lunch time) to discuss study or assignments. Many will not be interested but that's okay – starting with a small group is probably better. Use this group as the basis for your core success-support group.*

### Sharing with Adults

Sometimes your problems may be too 'big' for your friends or your friends just may not have a solution. Then it's time to share your problems with an adult. You may not like the idea of sharing your problems with an adult – you may feel shy or scared, or you may not know any adults you feel safe talking with – but this is something that you will need to develop if you wish to be successful in high school – and beyond.

You may not think so, but your parents (or parent) should be the first place to stop when sharing a problem. They know you and care about you and want you to be successful – believe it! In most cases, they will want to know how things are going with you (at school and at home) and the more you can share the better it will be. Sharing will make them feel better, too!

If you are unable to talk to your parents (for whatever reason) your teachers or coach should be the next stop. This is especially so for school–related issues but also for personal problems if there is a teacher you feel comfortable with. Remember, teachers are busy people and although they may want to help you they may not be able to all the time, so see them after class and arrange to meet with them later (lunchtime, after school, etc.) just like they would do with a parent. When you meet with them, share your problem and ask for some advice. If you are not comfortable talking to a teacher alone bring a friend along.

Finally, you may wish to talk with a chaplain or counsellor. Most schools have one or more of these and they are trained to help young people deal with their problems. If your school has chaplains or counsellors arrange to meet with one of them. Build a relationship with one that you feel comfortable with and see them on a regular basis if you are able – because the problems are not going to go away and a listening ear has great value.

- *ACTION – make a list of those adults whom you know and can trust enough to share your problems. If you have five or more you are very fortunate. Now, if you are able, go to each one and ask them if they would be willing to listen when you have a problem. They will usually say yes and then you can be confident of help when you need it.*

**Other Ways to Share**

Even if none of these suggestions work for you it is still vital that you share your problems with someone, and luckily it doesn't have to be a person. You can share your problems with God if you are religious – plenty of studies show that people who pray are happier and more stable. You can share your problems with a pet – talking to your dog may sound and look a little crazy, and your dog can't really give you advice, but it's the process of you talking that is the helpful part. If you are not religious and don't have a pet then at least share

19

your feelings in writing – a letter or diary. Writing it down will help you deal with your problems subconsciously. It's better than ignoring them or trying to 'soldier on' without help.

- *ACTION – purchase a small booklet and start a personal diary or journal. Each day write about what happened that day. Your journal could include the events, the problems, your thoughts and ideas, things that went well or didn't, or whatever you feel like writing. Keep the journal private. Try it for a month and see how much it improves your life.*

## Relaxation

If you want to be successful it is important that you are able to deal with pressure in positive ways. This is a skill that will help you in high school and beyond - the higher up you go, the more it will help you. There are a variety of ways to deal with pressure but most of them revolve around mastering the ability to relax. Relaxation is a powerful tool that will help you become successful. By relaxation I don't mean sprawling on the coach in front of the TV chewing on ice cream – that's 'veging', and it doesn't help you be successful! True relaxation is being in control of your body and emotions and not letting the stress overwhelm you.

### Being in the Moment

One important way that you can relax is to 'be in the moment' – that means being hyper-aware of yourself and your surroundings at a given moment. When you think about it much of what you stress about (assignments, tests, the issue with 'that' teacher, relationship hassles, etc.) all exist either in the past or in the future, not right now. If you can learn to escape to the moment you will be able to free yourself from stressful feelings that are not usually constructive. Being 'in the moment' helps you to separate yourself from your stress, balance yourself and reset yourself emotionally.

When you are 'in the now' your body and your mind are free from stress – and that is a good thing. Too much stress can have lots of negative impacts on your body and it's a good practise to reduce or eliminate the stress from your life – even if it's just for moments like this. You can be in the moment anytime and anywhere – on the bus, in bed, even in a test (just make sure you don't run out of time). Being in the moment may be difficult at first but the more you do it the easier and more beneficial it will be.

- *ACTION – Try this right now – close your eyes and focus on your other four senses: listen to the sound of the TV in the next room, or the dog barking across the road, listen to the sound of your breath flowing in and out of your nose; feel the weight of your body on the chair, the rising and falling of your chest, the air flowing into your lungs, the hardness of the book (or eReader) beneath your fingers; the taste of your saliva in your mouth, etc. Keep on doing this until the past and the future no longer exist – there is only 'now'. That's it.*

## Breathing

Another way to relax is to breathe. "Breathe? What do you think I've been doing all my life?" I hear you say. Well, I'm talking about deep, filling breaths. Scientists have determined that most people spend their lives breathing in quick, shallows breaths which fail to bring sufficient oxygen to the lungs and then the brain. This results in them feeling sluggish, less focused and less able to deal with stress. They are so used to shallow breathing that they don't realise they are doing it. Real, filling breaths take time and thought, but just a few of them can energise you for quite a while.

The amazing thing about deep breathing is that while you are doing it everything else disappears – it's like being in the moment but you are only breathing. Deep breathing fills your lungs with oxygen, which enables more oxygen to get to your brain, which makes your brain more effective and that, I'm guessing, is what you want!

You can complete a few deep breaths anywhere and anytime without drawing attention to yourself. Before you walk into that big test, take a few deep breaths; before you make that important presentation, take a few deep breaths; after the class with 'that teacher', take a few deep breaths. Note, deep breathing can help you prepare for stressful situations but it can also help you deal with stressful events.

- *ACTION – Stand or sit-up straight (you cannot do this slouching or lying down); close your mouth and take a deep breath slowly in through your nose and fill your lungs; hold the breath for about two seconds then slowly breath out through your mouth. Do this about three or four times. While you are breathing focus on your breath, focus on the air flowing in and out of your body. Feel how relaxed you are.*

**Prayer or Meditation**
Continuing in the same vein, prayer can help you relax and relieve stress. If you are religious you will be familiar with prayer. You will probably know that

sharing your problems with God can be very beneficial and often leads to answered prayers. What you may not be aware of is that studies have demonstrated that those people who pray and really believe in their prayers (and don't just do it because their parents do it) are more stable emotionally and more positive about life than those who don't. There's a lot to be said for regular, earnest prayer.

For those who aren't religious, meditation may be the answer. By meditation, I don't mean wearing a yellow robe and humming to yourself as you sit on the floor with your legs crossed. Meditation is simply an opportunity to clear your mind of distractions and cares for a few seconds or minutes. Just like with 'being in the moment' or deep breathing, to meditate you simply focus your mind on one thing – for example your breathing – until your surroundings slip away and you are in your own little world. It's about trying to force your body to be calm and relaxed. This has the effect of making your body calm and relaxed, which is a good thing – especially if you are going through something stressful. Meditation can be useful when you are trying to think clearly, but can't; when you need to make an important decision; or when your emotions are threatening to overwhelm you. A little bit of meditation will get you back on track and ready to face your challenges.

- *ACTION – take a few moments now to pray, say "Dear God, bring me peace and guidance as I develop positive habits of success. Help me learn and remember as I read this book and be able to find regular quiet times to pray".*

### Escapes

Another way to relax is to escape. No, I'm not talking about running away from home and backpacking around the world – to escape, you need to have a place you can go to or an activity you can do that helps you forget about the world and all its problems – at least for a while.

I have a number of things that I can do to escape from the stresses of my life: I sometimes play Halo on my Xbox or Civilization on my PC – when I'm playing a game I'm immersed in the world of the game and the real world disappears; I go for a walk listening to my favourite music or podcast – that helps me forget and get exercise at the same time; I watch one of my favourite Sci-Fi movies – you can't think about next week's problems when you're watching your hero save the world; I also go for long drives in my car. These things may or may not work for you but that's the point

– you must find the escapes that are good for you. It may be shooting baskets, running, or reading. Think about the places you go or the things you do that help you forget about your troubles. It's a good way to escape and recharge your batteries before getting back into the fray.

- *ACTION – What are your escapes? Think about the activities that have helped you to feel relaxed and stress-free, the activities that, whilst you were doing them you were not worried about anything. These are your escapes. Make a list of them and choose one of them when you need to 'get away'.*

## Walking

I just mentioned walking – it is one of the best ways to relax and relieve stress. Many studies have shown that it is also one of the best forms of exercise. Walking is good because you don't have to wear special 'walking clothes', you can do it on your way somewhere (such as school) and you can listen to music, an audiobook or a podcast while you do it.

*Audible.com or iTunes are great places to find an awesome range of audiobooks, or if you want free ones try Librevox.org for a great range of public domain audiobooks or check with most public libraries.*

I remember when I had a high-stress job running a high school – my day was often filled with stressful interactions with students, teachers and parents and by the end of it I had had enough. When I was able, I would leave the car at home so that I could walk home – which was perfect on those high-stress days. I would put an audiobook on, shut out the world and for 25 minutes I was stress-free. Plus, when I arrived home I could put the problems of the day away and not think about them until tomorrow. The walk made it easy to do that.

- *ACTION – Go for a walk right now. Make it a habit to go for a walk each day. Try to take a walk when you get home. Find a good podcast or audiobook and walk around the block. Aim for 30 minutes each day and you will find that not only do you feel more relaxed but you will get lots of 'reading' done.*

**Taking Breaks**
Taking breaks is also important if you want to relieve stress and relax. Many people believe that you will be successful if you work really hard all the time, and up to a point, that is correct. But most people don't know that

successful people know how to stop and take a break – this refreshes their mind and recharges their energy.

The longer you work without a break the less effective you become until eventually your work is so ineffective that you should not even bother (that's why all-night study doesn't work!). That is why professional athletes don't have too many games back-to-back, because they know they need to take a break to be at their best.

We will talk about study timetables later but before then it is important to build breaks into your days. This is vital now that we all work with screens. Staring at a computer or tablet screen can mesmerize you and not only your eyes dry out, but your brain does, too (we'll talk more about this later). So, whether it's 10 minutes every hour, or 5 minutes out of every 30, a regular break will help you to be your best.

- *ACTION – take a break right now. Stop reading and do something different – even if it's just standing up and walking to the kitchen to have a drink of water. When you return do you feel a little bit refreshed and more alert? That's power of breaks.*

# Positive Thinking

If you want to be successful you must be positive – it's as simple as that. Positive thinking can be the difference between achieving something and not. When you are positive about a situation you are more likely to approach that situation in the right frame of mind and get through it successfully, but if you aren't thinking positively then you will probably fail – even if you have the skills and knowledge. So how do you make positive thinking a part of you?

**Focus on the Positive**

Firstly, you must focus on the positive in a situation. You've probably heard the saying: "every cloud has a silver lining". This literally refers to dark clouds on a stormy day. Sometimes you can see a silvery glow around the edge of the dark clouds – that's the sun shining on the clouds from behind – showing that even when the day is stormy the sun is always there. That's what focusing on the positive means.

Always focusing on the positive in a situation is not easy – most people have fallen into the habit of seeing the negative side of a situation so it takes a lot of thought and practise to turn that around. By choosing to focus on the positive you are going against a lifetime of habit. Here are some examples:

- Your teacher brings a test forward one week. You could focus on the fact that you have one less week to study, or that once the test is finished you have an extra week to focus on other things.
- You lose your mobile phone and don't have enough money to buy a replacement. You could focus on all the things you're going to miss without your phone, or you could think about all the things you could achieve without the phone distracting you all the time.
- Your parents' car breaks down and you must wake up 45 minutes earlier to catch the bus to school. You could focus on the unfairness of the situation and the loss of sleep, or you could enjoy the opportunity to spend time reading a great book on your morning commute.

See, focusing on the positive in a situation is not easy – sometimes it's very difficult – but it can be done. In fact, the more you do it the easier it gets. And the more you do it the more positive you will feel about life. And the more positive you are about life the more positive life will become. It's not that positive people have better lives, but that they 'see' better lives, and often don't even notice the negative things that other people focus on.

There's a term called the 'self-fulfilling prophecy' which is related to focusing on positive things. A self-fulfilling prophecy is basically where a person believing that something will happen makes it happen. Here's an example: Fred believes that he's going to trip and fall over during the day – all day he is so focused on NOT tripping and falling over that he doesn't look where he's going and he trips and falls over. Or, another time when Fred is convinced that he will have a fight with his best friend – he is so tense about the fight he believes he's going to have that he offends his friend and they fight.

The self-fulfilling prophecy works with positive and negative thinking. If you think you will fail the test, you probably will. On the other hand, if you think you will pass the test you probably will – or at least there is a much better chance of it (assuming you've done the study, of course). The point is that your positive attitude is a vital requirement of success.

- *ACTION – make a list of ten negative events or influences in your life right now. Then focus on each one and try to think about what possible positive impact it could be having on your life. It may be difficult at first, but the more you exercise your 'positive muscle' the easier it will become.*

### Gratitude

Together with positive thinking is gratitude – being grateful for the things you have. Much study has been done on the benefits of gratitude. Being thankful actually improves your mood and makes you more likely to succeed, but just like positive thinking, gratitude must be practised – it doesn't come naturally.

To be grateful, you must first focus on the positive and then consider how blessed you are. Most people are in the habit of doing the opposite – they focus on the negative and then think about how hard their life is, how much of a victim they are. This is where the self-fulfilling prophecy kicks in – they feel like life is bad, they only focus on bad things and life becomes bad.

If you think about it you have a lot to be thankful for: that fact that you are even reading this book puts you in the most educated part of the world's population; the fact that you can afford to buy it puts you in the richest part of the population; the fact that you have a dry and safe place to read it makes you more privileged than most; and the fact that you want to be successful puts you ahead of most of the other people in your school. These are things to be grateful for – develop this habit of looking for things for which you can be grateful.

If you practise gratitude you will try to focus on the good things (even when things are not going well). Being grateful for all the good things in your life puts you in a positive frame of mind and enables you to see more good things. This builds up to a situation that is more conducive to success.

- *ACTION – using a small notebook or an app on your phone create a gratitude journal – a place where you list the things you are grateful for in your life. Each day, if you are able, think about the things that you are grateful for and list them in your journal. You will soon find that you have a lot to be grateful for.*

**Don't Worry**

Finally, if you want to stay positive you must learn not to worry about the things you cannot change. There are many things in life that we cannot change: the weather, the past, the thoughts and behaviour of others, and the list goes on... Too many people spend time and emotional energy thinking and worrying about all these things when it achieves very little.

For example, you had planned to spend the day outside with friends but the forecast is for rain – you can worry about what the weather will be like, but that will not change the weather, or you can plan for an alternative activity; You failed a very important test – you can beat yourself up and worry about the consequences but that cannot change the past, or you can work out what went wrong and find a remedy; you have a major assignment coming up but a local cinema has a marathon of your favourite movies this weekend – actually, that *is* something that you can change – plan to finish the first draft of the assignment before the weekend so that you have time to watch the marathon.

As you can see, it's important to know what you can change and what you cannot. Once you know that, you can focus your thoughts and energy towards those things that you can change and not those things you can't.

- *ACTION – think about a problem that you are currently facing in your life. Think about the causes of that problem. Think about what things would need to happen to possibly solve the problem. Do you have control over the solution? Are you able to contribute to eliminating the problem? If so, what can you do to make this happen? If not, try to convince yourself that if you can't control it there is no need to worry about it. Over time, this attitude will enable you to reduce your level of worry.*

# Motivation

A vital component of attitude when you are aiming for success is motivation. If you are not motivated, you will find completing your work to an acceptable standard very difficult, but if you are motivated there will be few obstacles that can stop you.

**Your Attitude**

Firstly, to motivate yourself you must have the right attitude – that's why we started this book by talking about attitude. The right attitude includes being confident in yourself and thinking positively. If you don't think you can do it you are not going to be motivated to do it, and if you think you will fail you will not want to try. So be confident and think positive and you will be more likely to want to get in there and get the job done.

**Your Reason**

Secondly, if you want to become and remain motivated you must consider your 'why?' This is your reason for wanting to do the task. In most cases your primary 'why' is going to be 'because you want to achieve top grades and succeed at high school'. There may be other 'whys' such as 'you want to impress your friends and make your parents proud' but success should be your main one. Remember, your 'why' should not be 'because your teacher told you to' – if you are relying on extrinsic motivation you are setting yourself up for failure. You should be motivated intrinsically, that is, the reasons come from within you so they cannot be taken away. You cannot really be motivated to do something unless you have good reasons for 'wanting' to do it.

**Your Goals**

Thirdly, you must ensure you that you know where you are going – a goal. We will discuss goals in more depth later, but for now it's important to know that being motivated is much better with a goal in mind. For example, if you have a test coming up you will be more motivated to study for it if you have a clear goal in mind – say a result of 90% (100% would be even better) – but any positive goal is going to make your study sessions more effective.

Write your goal as a statement of something you will achieve, and make it specific. For example, rather than just stating "get 90% on the Science test" you should state it as "I will achieve a grade of 90% in the Science test on Thursday." As you read this you will be training your mind to believe it, your confidence will grow and your study will be more effective.

It is also important for you to display your goal where you can see it as you work. This helps you in several ways: it motivates you, it keeps you focused, it helps you visualise the outcome you desire, and it keeps you accountable. A goal wall or board is one idea – you can even divide it up into short-term and long-term goals (more on that later). It is an idea to put your 'why' with your goals to make them more motivational. For example, rather than just displaying the goal "I will achieve a grade of 90% in the Science test on Thursday" you could add your 'why' "I will achieve a grade of 90% in the Science test on Thursday, because I hope to have a career in medicine when I graduate." When you know what your goal is and why you want it, you will be much more motivated to work towards and reach it.

- *ACTION – we will spend more time on goals later, but for now think about what you want to achieve for the next week. These goals can relate to school or home or something else. Come up with a few goals (five is a good number), write them down and focus on achieving these goals for the next week. After the week, assess whether setting the goals made it easier to achieve them.*

**Your Team**

Lastly, to stay motivated you need a team. Working towards something is much harder when you are doing it alone. When you have people working with you, who share your goals and also want to succeed, you are much more likely to succeed. Their motivation will push you, and your own motivation, in turn, will push them, and so on – a positive, upward spiral.

Earlier we talked about forming a study group. This is one of the best ways to keep yourself motivated and focused on success. An effective study group is formed of people who all want the same thing – academic success. Do not make the mistake of forming (or joining) a study group because the people are popular, or fun, or friends – unless they share your desire for success. If the whole group wants to succeed you will be motivated to work harder and your study will be more effective. Have the study group share goals so that you are all working towards the same things. Help each other, feed off each other's energy and motivate each other to achieve your goals.

- *ACTION – make a list of those people you know who would form a really effective study group. They don't need to be in the same class (or even in the same school) just willing and able to take part in a study group and motivated to succeed. Once you have the list, approach each person to gauge their interest.*

# Bullying

*NOTE: this section provides some strategies for overcoming bullying but it is advice only. If, at any time you are made to feel unsafe or in danger you must seek help from someone in authority as soon as possible!*

This section on bullying is included in this book of succeeding in high school because if you are focused on success there will probably be people who will despise you for it. It is important that your attitude is right when others attempt to bully you so that they will not get in the way of your success.

It is an unfortunate reality that in many schools if you are focused on academic success in high school you will be a target for bullies. This could be that, because they are low performers, bullies are jealous of your success; that your success makes them feel more inadequate; that academic success is not popular; or it may be their way of finding their own success. Whatever the reason, bullying is very difficult to take and, despite what a school's website may say, it is still very common.

When I was growing up I was smaller than my peers, a skinny little runt of a kid who was more at home reading under a tree than playing sports with the other boys. That made me a target and I responded by lashing out

39

physically. Rarely a week went by without me being involved in some sort of fight. Usually, it was when an older or bigger kid told me to move on and I told them in no uncertain terms to get lost. I rarely won those fights but eventually the school ground learned a healthy respect for the little kid who wouldn't back down. So I know what being bullied is like. I am certainly not advocating violence as an answer, and in these days of school shootings and stabbings it certainly causes more harm than good. Since that time, however, I have spent many hours counselling students and their parents about bullying and have found a simple strategy to help victims of bullying. It is called the Ha Ha So Strategy.

HA HA SO

The HA HA So Strategy is used in schools across the world as a defence against bullying. The Acronym H.A.H.A.S.O. stands for the steps involved in defeating the bullying attempt but also demonstrates the dismissive attitude that needs to be adopted by those being bullied – as in "Ha, ha, so what, I don't care!" Often, when bullies know that they can't 'get under your skin' they will move on to 'softer' targets. So here's the acronym:

**H** = **Help** – get help – especially if you feel physically in danger. Help may be found in friends (remember, safety in numbers), teachers (or chaplains, counsellors, coaches, etc.) or family members (parents, siblings, etc.). It is important to get help but try not to get someone else to solve the problem for you – if they do you will learn nothing!

**A** = **Assert Yourself** – it is important that you stand up for your rights and safety. In many cases bullies will not be used to being challenged or confronted. Just ensure that you stand up for your rights without challenging their manhood, strength or abilities, etc. If that happens they may need to escalate the confrontation to save face. Make your response clear and strong – "Excuse me! Why don't you leave us/me alone? I don't like being bullied, and it doesn't help any one!"

**H** = **Humour** – Making a joke out of the situation or confrontation is often a good way to dissipate the tension. Something simple like: "Knock, knock." No one could resist responding with "Who's there?" "Boo!" "Boo Who?" "Oh, don't cry, I'm sure things will get better!" Just ensure that your joking doesn't offend or belittle the bully, or anyone else.

**A** = **Avoid** – An effective way to defend against bullying is to avoid them when possible. If the bullies are always

41

hanging around a certain place don't go there unless you must. If there is an alternate route, take it.

**S = Self-talk** – This doesn't mean talking to yourself out loud – that's just asking for attention. Self-talk is when you reassure yourself (in your mind) that you are okay, that there is nothing wrong with you, that the fault is with the bully, not you. Remember that bullies act the way they do because they feel insecure about themselves. Tell yourself that and you will feel more confident to deal with them.

**O = Own it** – this means agreeing with what the bully says – that gives them nothing else to say. For example, "Yeah, I am a bit stupid, that's why I study so much – so that I can keep up", or "I know this is a bad haircut – I really want to make sure my photo doesn't appear in the school newsletter." It doesn't have to be true for you to own it, just use it as a strategy to deflect the bully and then move on.

These strategies can be used individually or in combination, such as asserting yourself with humour, or owning it with self-talk. Sometimes these strategies may not work but that doesn't mean they are useless. If it doesn't work in one situation, it may work in another. The point is to keep trying to take control of the situation so that you are not at the mercy of the bully.

It is important not to let bullies get in the way of your success. They may be bigger and more popular while at school but if you focus on your success the rewards will come to you, and not them.

- *ACTION – The HA HA SO Strategy will be much more effective if you are able to practise it often. If you witness someone else being bullied (and you don't feel safe stepping in) rehearse in your mind how you would use the Ha Ha So Strategy to disarm the situation. If you are bullied, but you didn't use the Ha Ha So Strategy spend some time after school going through the situation again so that you will be more prepared the next time it happens. The more you practise it the more prepared you will be.*

## Attitude Action Plan

1. Make the conscious decision right now to believe in yourself and your abilities – even if you are not yet certain what they are.
2. Think about the people in your life whom you can talk to. Resolve to share a problem with one of them each day.
3. Stop and breathe, right now – thinking about nothing but your breath. Do this a few times each day.

4. What are five things that you are grateful for, right now? Think about them for a few minutes and write them down.
5. What motivates you – consider your 'why'. Dwell on it for a few minutes and its importance to you.

# Part 2 – Lifestyle

You are probably, at this very moment, asking why I am now discussing lifestyle in a book about succeeding in high school. That's a very good question and the answer is very important, and something that is missed by so many people aiming for academic success. The reality is that your brain is not sitting in a jar up on the shelf – it's in your body and the healthier your body is the healthier your brain will be.

As the old saying goes: "healthy body, healthy mind", and it's true. Let's look at the biology for a moment: your brain is the most important organ in your body and it's also the thirstiest/hungriest. Your brain needs more blood (which carries nutrients and oxygen) than any other organ in the body – that's what those carotid arteries in your neck are doing. So, the healthier your body is, the better your circulation will be, the more effectively your heart will be able to pump blood through your arteries, and the more efficiently your arteries will be able to transport that vital blood to your brain. With a good supply of blood your brain will be able to process better. Simple, isn't it?

It is important to remember that a healthy lifestyle is about balance. Don't make the mistake of overdoing something healthy. Exercise is good for you but if you do too much it will cause injury; fruit is good for you but if you ate only fruit you would miss vital nutrients – see? Balance. So now we are going to spend some time looking at the best ways to create a lifestyle that is going to most effectively help you be successful.

*NOTE: Once again, this information is based upon many studies that have been done over the years but you should make sure you do your own research, including checking with health professionals, before you make dramatic changes to your lifestyle. This is doubly so if there are health considerations which are relevant for you.*

## Diet

Probably one of the most important factors in a healthy lifestyle is diet – and by 'diet' I don't mean eating only beans for the next two weeks, or whatever. By diet, I mean what you eat on a regular basis – your normal food and drink consumption. Unfortunately, many young people put taste before nutritional value when it comes to what they eat. If you wish to be successful you need to be a little more discerning. Following are some important changes that need to be made to ensure your body is at its peak.

### Drink more Water

Firstly, drink plenty of water. A large proportion of your brain is water. It is filled with and surrounded by a fluid which protects it and ensures it's working at peak performance. When you drink water, you replenish that fluid and keep your brain operating well. When you don't drink water, or you drink other fluids, that fluid becomes viscous and your brain becomes sluggish – you know that feeling you get in the afternoon when you find it difficult to think – that's often dehydration!

Dehydration also thickens your blood and makes it harder for nutrients and oxygen to be transported around the body. That's why they get you to drink water before you donate blood. Scientists have demonstrated that a drop in the body's hydration of only 2% can lead to significant brain impairment. Any higher can lead to coma and death! That's how important water is to your health.

When discussing the importance of drinking water, you may hear some people say, "but I don't need to drink water, I drink _____ (insert any drink besides water)". The truth is that only water benefits the body. Other drinks contain sugars, salts and other elements/chemicals that may act as a diuretic – a solution which removes moisture from the body. The more of these drinks you consume the more dehydrated you become. That is why most people live a dehydrated life without knowing it – they think they are drinking to hydrate when in fact they are not.

So, successful people drink mostly water. That doesn't mean you can drink only water (although that wouldn't be such a bad idea) it just means that you should make water your main drink and use everything else to supplement water. I would go so far as to recommend that you avoid soft drinks (such as Coca-Cola, Pepsi, etc.) completely because they contain way too much sugar; avoid drinks like coffee and tea because they are diuretics and can be addictive; minimise fruit drinks, because they also contain too much sugar; and keep energy drinks for when you are exercising only – not for a boost when you are studying.

If you are not used to drinking water you can increase your motivation by adding a few squeezes of orange or lemon juice (real, not packaged) to your glass of water. Note that a side effect of drinking more water is an increased need to visit the toilet, but that's a good thing – not only will does it signify healthy kidneys, it also makes you get up more, another benefit, as we'll see when we discuss exercise.

- *ACTION – buy a water bottle and sit in on your desk. Fill it up with water right now and keep drinking it. When it's empty, refill it and keep drinking. Make this a habit.*

## Eat less Sugar

The second improvement that can be made to your diet is to reduce, or even better, eliminate sugar from your life. A lot of study has been done on the impact of sugar on human physiology. From the body's perspective sugar can have an effect like that of heroin or cocaine, and it can be addictive, too. When we eat something with refined sugar in it our body likes it and craves more. When it doesn't get more, it goes into a 'withdrawal' and sends signals to the brain saying, "get me more of that stuff!" Why do you think you can never only eat only one chocolate-chip cookie? It's those cravings. After getting the 'sugar rush' your body will drop into a type of depression that leaves you flat and lacking energy. Most people never realise they have developed a craving for sugar because they keep eating it and satisfying their body's need for it, but those people who suddenly stop taking sugar report cravings, increased agitation, even depression and the shakes. Obviously, these are extremes but it is important to know what impact sugar has on us.

49

You may be asking, why avoid sugar? How is this going to make me more successful in high school? Well, remember that we want to be our best. The problem with sugar is that it reduces the overall effectiveness of your body. Not only has too much sugar been clearly linked to diabetes but it has also been shown that sugar does directly and indirectly impact your thought processes. Sugar makes you more open to suggestion and less prone to processing deeply – in effect it makes you stupid and lazy. Obviously, you are not going to turn into a moron after having one bowl of ice-cream but these effects are cumulative and a lifetime of sugar consumption is going to have an effect.

- *ACTION – do you have a 'sweet tooth'? Resolve right now to reduce the amount of sugar you ingest and share your resolution with friends and family. If they can support you it will be much easier to reduce and eventually eliminate sugar from your diet.*

### Eat more Fruit and Vegetables

The third way to improve your diet is to eat more fruit and vegetables. Fruit and vegetables provide many benefits to ensure you are at your best: They have natural sugars with the advantages of fibre; they fill you up without adversely affecting your weight; they have

50

all the vitamins and minerals you need to keep your body in peak condition; and fruit (and some vegetables) is easy – just grab and eat. A diet of primarily fruit and vegetables (ensure it has good variety) will make you more energetic and enable you to think clearly without needing supplements or 'boosters'.

Many studies have shown that the less meat you consume the better it is for your body. We are told that we need meat for protein but the reality is that some vegetables provide more protein per gram than meat. Besides that, meat (and other animal products) is the sole source of cholesterol and has no fibre for the body. So, a diet with a minimum of meat is better for you. If you feel you cannot live without meat then restrict your meat intake to a couple of meals a week with the rest of them being vegetable-based. You will notice an improvement in your energy levels and performance.

- *ACTION – get up and grab some fruit right now – none in the house? Speak to your parents (or whomever does the grocery shopping) and ask them to add more fruits and vegetables to the shopping list because you are resolving to eat more fruit and vegetables. Don't just say it – mean it!*

**Always eat Breakfast**

The fourth way to improve your diet is to always eat breakfast. Breakfast is called the most important meal of the day, but it is the one which is missed most often. Breakfast is important because it is the first meal of the day (it breaks your overnight fast – 'fast' meaning go without eating – that's why it's called break-fast) and it is the meal that gives you the push to get through the day. If you miss breakfast you will be behind the action for the rest of the day. Also, mornings are usually the most productive times so that is when you need your energy.

If you are tempted to miss breakfast (either because you are late, want to sleep in, or are watching your weight) remember the following: studies have shown that people who regularly miss breakfast perform worse at school or work, enjoy their day less and are more prone to weight gain than those who do not miss breakfast regularly. If you are serious about being successful at high school you must make eating breakfast a habit. It doesn't have to be a big affair, in fact, a simple meal of whole grain cereal with fruit is adequate. Even some toast is better than nothing!

- *ACTION – check the food cupboards – what is in there that you can use for breakfast tomorrow?*

*Plan your breakfast before you go to bed –*
*actually take out the elements that you plan to*
*eat and lay them out on the table ready for the*
*next morning (check that this is okay with the*
*rest of the family, first). If you physically set out*
*the components of an action you will be more*
*likely to follow through.*

### Avoid Junk Food

Diet improvement number five is an obvious one, but needs to be stated anyway – avoid junk food. Junk food is anything that has been processed (that is, comes in a box or wrapper) which contains 'empty calories'. Empty calories provide you with energy but little or no nutrition. Chocolate bars, chips, and sugary snacks are all junk food and they are good only for a short 'hit' of energy, not for sustained vitality. This 'sugar hit' provides a sudden spike of energy followed by a sudden drop. I will sometimes snack on a chocolate bar when I'm doing some physical work or exercising because that is when the body could use the extra energy, but junk food is not what the body needs when you are sitting still.

Unfortunately, junk food has become a habit for those of us in the West. When we are doing something and we get the urge to 'munch' we usually reach for junk food. Instead, keep something healthy within reach when you are studying or relaxing, like nuts, apples or carrot sticks, these still satisfy the munching urge but are much better for you and will not give you a sugar high. Making the healthy alternative a habit will make it easier to avoid junk food and keep your body working at its best.

- *ACTION – Before you make any changes to what you eat keep a food journal for a week to monitor what your diet is really like. Include everything you eat and drink, times and amounts. After the week examine your journal and identify what bad habits have developed. Determine the one (yes, only one) change that you can make to improve your diet. Do that for a month, then keep another food journal for a week and repeat the process. After a year, your diet will have improved dramatically without too much pain.*

## Exercise

Exercise is vital to your success, and although it may sound like a contradiction, you must exercise if you wish to be successful at high school. We've already looked at the importance of keeping your body operating at peak efficiency through what you eat, and exercising it is just as important. Remember when we talked about the brain's need for blood – blood gets to the brain through the pumping of your heart and your heart pumps best when you are moving. People who exercise regularly increase the capacity of their heart to pump blood – even when they are not exercising – so the benefits of exercise continue after you've finished.

Conversely, those people who are sedentary have a heart that must work harder to pump blood. Studies show that sedentary people are generally more stressed, get sicker and injured more often, are more prone to weight gain, lack energy, don't sleep as well and are less happy. Overall, it's a dark picture if you don't exercise.

What do I exactly mean by exercise? Well, I don't mean that you should run ten kilometres every day and a marathon each weekend – although if that's what you want to do then go for it. By exercise I mean 'staying active'. Too many of our modern hours are spent sitting down – we sit at school, we sit on the bus, we sit at home, etc. That puts our body into a rest state which is not good for you when it is sustained for long periods. Being active means you are doing something physical on a regular basis. Yes, you should become involved in some type of sport (cricket, soccer, volleyball, swimming, whatever, a few times each week. But even if you already are, you should still try to break up sitting with some activity.

Too much stress is something that you should avoid, and as we have already discussed, exercise is one way to reduce your stress. An exercising body releases chemicals (endorphins) which make you feel better, the physical exertion makes you breath deeper (we've looked at the benefits of that), and the heart pumps more blood through your system, which helps to clear out all the rubbish in your body.

So, exercise has a very positive impact on your body, but it also has a good mental influence. When you get involved in exercise it helps you to refocus your thoughts and clear out your mind. Anyone who has gone for a long run, bike ride or hike will know that once you get started the worries that have been consuming you drift away and seem less important. This gives your mind time to rest and refocus your thoughts, and it refreshes your ideas. You will usually find that after exercising you are more ready to tackle the challenges of your life than you were before. Involve yourself in exercise regularly and you will find that stress will become less of a problem for you.

Scientists have known for quite a while that exercise increases immunity, hence if you exercise regularly you will not be sick as much, if at all. I know of people who are sick all the time: if it's not the flu, it's a cold, if it's not a cold, it's the sniffles, if it's not the sniffles, it's something else. Rarely a week passes without them catching something. They are usually miserable and lacking in energy and enthusiasm – not a great recipe for success! I, on the other hand, rarely get sick (maybe a couple of days of flu-like symptoms once a year) and I have a lot more energy than many people my age. This is due to two factors: diet (which we have already discussed) and exercise.

The science of it is (very basically) that when your body moves on a regular basis, chemicals are released that make it stronger against germ-invaders. And, your increased heart capacity makes transporting your blood defences around your body quicker and easier. The bottom line is that the more regularly you exercise the healthier you will be.

An obvious reason to exercise is to reduce, or maintain, weight. If you were to exercise regularly (and eat well – remember, this is all connected) you would find that weight gain would be less of an issue for you. That doesn't mean that you will never have to think about your weight – that's something that many of us need to watch our whole life – but it does mean you won't have to worry about it.

As already mentioned exercise increases your energy levels. That may sound like a contradiction – use energy to exercise and increase your energy levels. The fact is that your body was made to move and when it does it performs better. Look at it this way, a guy who runs every day is going to have more energy than another guy who doesn't, right? If you asked both guys to run around the block, who is going to be able to do it with energy to spare? The runner, obviously. It's the same with you. The more you exercise the more energy you will have.

Note that when you start to exercise you should start small and build your way up. That means if you've never run before don't make your first run 10 kilometres – try a run around the block and then increase it a little bit each day. Also, be aware that when you first start to exercise you will be tired because your body is not used to it – it will take time to adapt – so for a while you will feel like you have less energy, but when your body has adapted your energy levels will increase and you will be able to achieve so much more each day. Not only will your body work better but your brain will, too.

Another important benefit of exercise is improved sleep. We will talk about the importance of sleep next, but for now, all you need to know is that sleep is vital for the health of your body and especially your brain. Have you ever lay down to sleep and just couldn't? There were too many ideas crashing around in your head – the day's issues crowding to get attention from your tired brain. You lay there for what seemed like hours until you finally drifted off into a restless sleep, only to wake up feeling like you hadn't slept at all. Sound familiar?

When you exercise on a regular basis you will find that you fall asleep quicker and sleep more restfully. It's a natural consequence of physical exercise. Ensure that you don't exercise too close to bedtime and you should develop a habit of sleeping easier.

- *ACTION – Just like you have kept a food log to keep track of the food you eat, start an exercise log to keep track of how physically active you are. Keep it for a week and record all your activity in it. Categorise each activity as Active – you are moving around physically, and Inactive – you are sitting down. At the end of the week examine the results and determine how much of your time is spent being inactive. Is there room to improve? If yes, how? Use the results to develop exercise habits for yourself.*

## Sleep

We've just mentioned the importance of sleep to your success, particularly when you are in high school. It is an unfortunate reality that most high school students do not get enough sleep. With TV, computers, games, messenger apps, texting and music there is simply too much to keep you awake – and that doesn't even include school work. The average is somewhat less than six hours sleep per night, but scientists have found that teenagers need at least seven hours, and some up to nine or ten per night. That's a lot of lost sleep. So why is sleep so important?

Sleep is the body's way to recharge and repair – while you are dreaming of the holidays, your body is working very hard to get you ready for the next day. Much of your growth takes place when you sleep, your memories are programmed in and your subconscious processes the events of the day. Without sleep, or with not enough, you would (besides feeling tired) think slower, remember less and be generally weaker. In fact, sleep is so important to us that sleep deprivation is used as torture by some countries, and without it a person will eventually go insane and die – even if they have everything else they need!

To succeed at high school, you are going to need to concentrate, and for your brain to concentrate at its peak you are going to need sleep. Numerous studies have demonstrated that lack of sleep leads to reduced concentration. In fact, it can be so profound that some compare lack of sleep to being affected by alcohol. That's right, if you turn up to school without getting enough sleep you may as well be drunk – not a recipe for success!

The impact of not enough sleep is not usually noticeable until it's serious. Yes, everybody is aware that when you have not had enough sleep you yawn and feel tired, but what most people are not aware of is the impact it has on your thinking processes – they are slower and less precise. It has even been shown that a consistent lack of sleep actually reduces a person's I.Q. – makes them dumber! Hopefully you can now see the importance of sleep to your brain.

Another reason to get enough sleep is for your body's immunity. We've already discussed the importance of being healthy and sickness-free to succeed at high school and the best way to achieve that (besides a good diet and exercise) is by sleeping enough each night. A decent night's sleep will give you more energy and make your body more immune to common illnesses that are in the neighbourhood. That doesn't mean that you will never get sick, but it does mean you will get sick much less than if you didn't get enough sleep.

I have seen this happen in my own life – if there have been days when I didn't get enough sleep (usually a week or so of late nights and early mornings) I would get the flu – it would happen without fail. If I felt my throat begin to get sore and my head start to throb I knew that my immunity was down and I was catching something. If I was quick I would spend the next couple of nights getting a good night's sleep and it would clear up. It was like clockwork!

A longer-term result of healthy sleeping is effective brain development. Scientists have shown that much of the brain's growth and development takes place when you sleep, and this continues until well after you have completed high school. In fact, brains keep developing until well into an individual's twenties, and for everyone sleep is a time when the brain maintains itself and processes information. That means that if you are doing without sleep now your brain will not be developing as it should be and will not reach the capacity that it can. This could have serious consequences later in your life.

All those people that you know who stay up late are doing themselves irreparable damage.

To be successful you need to ensure that you are getting a good night's sleep regularly. That doesn't mean that you must go to bed early every night – sometimes a late night cannot be avoided – but it does mean that you should develop the habit of getting the sleep that you need most nights. It's the regular sleep loss that can do damage.

## How to get a Good Night's Sleep

So now that you know how important sleep is to your success how do you ensure that you can get a good night's sleep? Today's typical house contains so many distractions that getting enough sleep is difficult. It won't happen naturally – you will have to take actions to purposefully make sleep easier. Try the following strategies:

### Regular Sleep Time

Establish a regular sleep time and try to keep to it as much as possible. By a regular sleep time I mean making your time for sleep the same each night. When you establish a pattern your body becomes familiar and comfortable with it. If you go to bed at around the same time each night you will find it easier to fall asleep. If you go to bed at a different time each night your body will not know that it's time for sleep and falling asleep will be more difficult. This is also true of weekends – don't make the mistake of going to sleep much later on weekends because that will upset your sleep 'habit'.

## Avoid Stimulants

You should avoid taking stimulants a few hours before your time for sleep. Coffee is an obvious one, but you should also avoid energy drinks and drinks with lots of sugar (soft drinks). A mistake which many people make is taking drinks to 'keep them awake' while they work or study and then they have trouble going to sleep. If you must take stimulants (I generally don't recommend it!) do it earlier in the day so that they do not interfere with your sleeping. Also, if you are so tired that you need to take stimulants then it's a pretty clear message from your body to stop and sleep – you should listen.

*NOTE: later when we talk about organisation and study habits you will see that there is really no need for those late-night study sessions.*

## Noise

Reducing or eliminating noise is another way that you can increase your chances of a good night's sleep. Too much noise is not only a distraction – making it harder to fall asleep – it can also prevent you from falling into the deeper REM sleep, which is vital for all the brain repair activity we talked about earlier.

You may not have control over some noises (such as trains or traffic) but the ones you can control should be minimised. If you need to wear earmuffs for sleeping, install thick curtains to muffle the noise or play 'white noise' music which helps block out other noises then do so. Also, don't make the mistake of thinking that listening to your own music will help – it will keep you awake and prevent you from getting a decent sleep.

### Electronics

These days, one of the biggest enemies of good sleep is the 'dreaded screen'. This includes TVs, phones, tablets and computers. The problem with electronic screens is that (besides being a distraction that can keep you awake) they emit a 'blue light' which prevents your body from preparing for sleep.

Biologically, when your body perceives that it's time to sleep it releases chemicals which slow your body down and make it ready for 'shutdown'. When you are staring at a screen your body is perceiving the light in the same way as it sees daylight and it sends a very clear message that it's not time for sleep. So, when you finally put your screen away your body is not ready for rest and it becomes hard to fall asleep.

Make it a habit to turn off and put away your 'screens' before you get into bed. If you 'need' to check your friends' status or the latest posts do so earlier in the evening, and not before you try to sleep. Don't stress – it will all be there in the morning! Also, if you can, turn off notifications on your phone. The worst thing that you can do for a good night's sleep is to have your phone beeping and buzzing every few minutes all night. It will prevent REM sleep and you will not get the rest you need. After all, what's more important – catching the latest cat video as soon as it's posted online or your own success now and in the future?

### Light

To get the best sleep, try to make your room as dark as possible. Remember what I said earlier about the effect of light on your body? If your room is dark you will be able to fall asleep and drift into a deep sleep faster. If there is light in the room it will take you longer to fall asleep and the sleep will not be as deep or beneficial.

Light sources that can be a problem include: daylight, if the sun sets late where you are and the light comes in through the window your body will still think it's time to be active; screen light, we've already discussed the impact of this on your body; and artificial light, this includes any sort of globe or light source such as candles or lamps (including LEDs). Even the light from a bedside clock radio can impact sleep quality. The one exception to this may be fire – as in an open fire place. The warmth and natural rhythms of fire are soothing and promote sleep, but unless you have a fireplace in your bedroom I do NOT recommend lighting a fire before you go to sleep.

To prevent these light sources interrupting your sleep you can try the following: install thick, dark curtains or shutters – or at least something that blocks out all outside light; if you do have electronic light sources that cannot be removed, such as clocks, ensure that they are covered or not facing your bed; keep your phone face down and turn off notifications so that you are not drawn to it throughout the night; use a sleep mask (over your eyes) to keep out light if there is no other way. Discover which of these you can manage and your body/brain will thank you.

### Be Positive and Happy

This may not seem relevant at first, but being positive and happy will help you sleep better. Remember when we talked about the brain and the power of positive thinking? This also works for sleeping better. When you are feeling positive (about things in general or something specific) your body is more relaxed than when you are stressed about something. In the same way, feeling happy is better than feeling angry or upset about something. In an angry state, your body is tense and sleep will be difficult. There are some exceptions to this but generally happy people sleep better.

To achieve a mindset that is conducive to sleep ensure that you do not go to sleep when you are angry or upset – take a hot bath or shower, go for a long walk, listen to relaxing music or do anything that is going to help you unwind the tension. This will enable you to fall asleep faster and sleep better.

**Have a Sleep Process**

A sleep process is a series of actions, which you develop into a habit, leading to sleep. When you have developed a sleep process that is carried out every night you will find going to sleep much faster and easier. The sleep process is effective because the body becomes used to doing things in a particular way – think about how you brush your teeth or dry yourself after a shower – this is called 'muscle memory' and it makes repetitive actions easier. When you put a series of actions together and end them with sleep your body will remember and whenever you carry out those actions your body will automatically prepare for sleep.

Some examples of a sleep processes include:

1.  Have a warm shower, brush your teeth, put on your pyjamas, wish your family good night, say a prayer, read for 15 minutes, sleep.
2.  Do 10 push-ups and 10 sit-ups, get a drink of cold water, do breathing exercises for 5 minutes, read for 15 minutes, sleep.
3.  Shut down your computer, turn all lights off except the bedside light, have a drink of warm milk, play some relaxing music softly, meditate for 10 minutes, write in your gratitude journal, read for 10 minutes, sleep.

What makes up the process is less important that the process itself, assuming, of course, that the activities you choose do not wake you up. It's the process, repeated each night, which readies your body for sleep and ensures that you will get a good night's rest. A sleep process may also have the advantage of making a series of positive actions habits that you carry out each night, rather than just occasionally.

- *ACTION – create a sleep process. Think about the activities that you could carry out each night that will make it easier to fall sleep – they must be things that you enjoy but cannot be exciting or stimulating (no screens)! Try to include reading in your process, it's good to get into the habit of daily reading and reading is very conducive to sleep (who hasn't fallen asleep whilst reading?) — just ensure that you're not up until 3am because you can't put the book down! Once you've developed your process write it down and leave it near your bed — this will help you be consistent until the habit sticks. If it doesn't work try to modify it until you find something that does. Keep at it for at least a month, then it should be a part of your life.*

## Emotions

*NOTE: this section has some general and basic advice regarding your emotional wellbeing and how that can relate to your success. This information should not be used to diagnose or treat depression, chemical imbalances or other serious emotional issues. If you have questions or find that you cannot control your emotions you should seek professional medical assistance.*

Your emotions are an important part of who you are — they can assist you or get in the way of your success. The trick is to control your emotions (as much as possible) and use them to your advantage. It's easy to say but difficult to do. Let's look at some ways that we can ensure that your emotions do not get in the way of your success.

## Take Control

It may sound like I'm trying to turn you into a Vulcan (remember Mr Spock from Star Trek) by advising you to control your emotions, but I'm not (although being a Vulcan would certainly help in some situations, wouldn't it?). Controlling your emotions doesn't mean eliminating your emotions. Emotions are helpful and expressing them in constructive ways is healthy. The problems arise when we lose control of our emotions and they take control of us. Have you ever been in a situation where you are so angry or upset that you can't control what you are saying? That's losing control of your emotions and it rarely ends well.

So how do you control your emotions? Firstly, acknowledge what emotions you have trouble controlling. You may lose your temper a lot, or cry a lot when you are upset – whatever it is once you acknowledge it, you will be closer to controlling it. Talk to those people who are closest to you (family and friends) and ask them if there are any of your emotions that seem to be out of control sometimes. Once you have identified an out of control emotion you can begin to 'tame' it.

To help you control your emotions try the following:

- Using visualisation techniques (discussed earlier) picture yourself in a situation which would normally set you off but see yourself controlling the emotion you usually lose;
- Use deep breathing, meditation or prayer to 'centre' yourself with particular focus on the emotion that is causing you trouble;
- Create a controlled response for when you feel the emotion starting to increase. This may include counting, repeating a poem or rhyme or doing something physical like placing your hands on your head or face, or snapping a rubber band around your wrist. These actions have no meaning in themselves but they can 'distract' your emotion and allow your conscious self to regain control.

Whichever you choose (or anything else you can come up with to help you control your emotions) ensure you use it regularly so that keeping your emotions in check becomes easier.

### Be Happy

You probably don't remember the song "Don't Worry, Be Happy!" that was big years ago. It was a simple song but the idea behind it was very profound. Being happy is an important concept that many successful people understand. Most people think of happiness as something that you feel when good things happen to you, but in fact happiness is a choice – you can choose to be happy or sad – regardless of what is happening to you.

There is a close link between your emotions and your physiology – your body. For example, when you are feeling depressed your posture is bent over, your face is downcast, your eyes and mouth more closed and your skin takes on a pale appearance – a physiological expression of that emotion. In contrast, when you are feeling happy your posture is straighter, your face upward-looking, your eyes are open and shining, in fact your whole face is usually glowing with joy. This simple example shows how are bodies are linked to our emotions.

The question is: do our emotions cause our body to change or does our body cause our emotions to change? Try this simple experiment – think about something that depresses you; notice the 'heaviness' that comes over you. If you continue to dwell on that depressing thing your body would respond and soon you would be depressed. Now, smile! Physically move your mouth into a smiling position (edges of your mouth pointing upwards, teeth showing – I mean a real, happy smile!) Can you feel your whole face changing? Your cheeks rise, your eyes open more – can you feel your mood changing? Hopefully you can. This is a very simple demonstration of how changing our body can change our mood, and how you CAN change what you feel.

So now that you know that you can change how you feel it is important to choose to be happy. It's related to the positive thinking we were discussing earlier – you cannot expect to be successful when you are often negative about things.

- *ACTION – create a gratitude journal – a booklet where you daily list all the things for which you are grateful – it's a great way to maintain your perspective and stay positive.*

**Your Music**
Music is closely related to emotions. If you don't believe me think about your favourite songs – how do they make you feel? Do some make you pumped, while others make you feel gloomy? Rock songs make you energised, while love songs make you yearn for friendship? This is not accidental. Songs are designed to reach the emotional places of a person – that's how they sell more songs! The more you feel, the more you buy! Cynical, but true.

This fact makes it very important to choose your music carefully. You might ask what your choice of music has to do with success in high school and that's a good question. The answer is not popular but is backed by much scientific evidence. The bottom line is that there is some music which is helpful to you and some which is not. For example, listening to relaxing music when you are planning to workout would be counter-productive, and in the same way listening to heavy, beat-filled rock when you are trying to study or relax for sleep would not help.

Think about the music you listen to and when you listen to it. Is some of it just habit – you walk into the room and turn on the radio? Is some of it what your friends have shared with you and it's not really you? The point is that you should be thinking about the music you listen to and what impact it is having on you – how it is affecting your emotions. When you can do that you will be more in control of your emotions.

- *ACTION – list the first ten songs that come into your head. Are they songs that you listen to regularly? Are they songs that you listen to because you like them or because your friends like them? Be honest – no one will look at this but you. How many of the ten songs would you continue to listen to if no one even knew? How many would you stop listening to? By reflecting on your music habits like this you can better define your own tastes.*

**Your Friends**

Just like the music you listen to, your friends can have a major impact on you and your emotions. Do you have some friends who make you laugh and feel happy, while others are always serious and make you feel depressed? If so, then you know how friends impact you. Just like with your music, it is important to be aware of your friends and analyse how they are impacting you.

Be aware that I am not presuming to tell you who you should, or should not, have as friends. I'm just trying to get you to look at your friends objectively for a moment so that you can see how they change you. Remember, you are all about your success, and you should be doing all that you can to ensure that you are successful – that includes making sure your friends are making it easier for you, not harder.

Let's look at a couple of examples: say you have a friend called Jane. She is lots of fun, always joking, and great to be around. She is also not too interested in succeeding at high school. She is more interested in having fun and enjoying the moment. Then there's Stella. She is also good to be around, but for different reasons. Stella enjoys reading and outdoor sports. When she is not stuck in some Shakespeare play she is training for a half marathon. She has big ambitions for when she has finished high school and works hard to reach her goals.

Although you enjoy the company of both these girls and you consider both your friends, which of them do you think is going to assist you in becoming successful? Obviously, Stella is going to be the friend that will help you reach success. Does that mean that you should stop being friends with Jane? Of course not! Jane can still be your friend but when you acknowledge that success is important to you Stella will be your first preference. When you must choose between spending time with Jane or Stella think about where each of them will lead you. Remember, your friends have a powerful influence on you – the more time you spend with them the stronger the influence – so you need to be aware of how you are being influenced. The best way to do this is to choose your friends carefully.

All the most successful people acknowledge that, in business, if you wish to be successful you should surround yourself with people who are going to help you reach your goals. Life is no different – you should surround yourself with people who are going to help you be successful. If most of your friends are interested only in having fun you will soon be focusing on that and success will pass you by. On the other hand, if your friends are also interested in success you will be able to help each other reach it.

- *ACTION – make a list of your top ten friends. For each one, ask the following questions: Am I totally comfortable with this person? Is this person interested in my success? Is this person interested in their own success? Does this person encourage or discourage positive study habits in me? Once again, be honest – you will be the only person seeing your answers to these questions.*

**Exercise**

The final way to take control of your emotions is to make exercise a part of your life. We've already looked at how important exercise is to your success, and the benefits that it has for your mind, but it can also benefit your emotional health. Studies have shown that those who exercise on a regular basis are happier and more emotionally stable than those who don't. Of course, there are many other factors that determine emotional health but exercise has been shown to have a significant positive impact on it.

Exercise can help in many ways: When you are feeling like your emotions (anger, fear, loneliness, etc.) are getting the better of you some exercise can usually ease those feelings. A quick run around the block, a swim, a short cycle ride or a session with a punching bag will often help you to focus and get through the overwhelming feelings. Regular exercise can also help to reduce the times that you feel overwhelmed by those feelings.

So how does exercise help? When you exercise, your body releases chemicals which make you feel better and help to overcome those feelings of anger, fear, etc. Remember, those feelings are simply chemicals in your body and if you can change your body chemistry (in a healthy, positive way) you will be able to overcome those feelings – that's what exercise does. Exercise also has the benefit of being a distraction – I know that when I am riding my bike, swimming or taking part in some other intense activity I will focus on what I am doing and the issues that have been worrying me fade away – at least for a while. After the exercise, they do not seem as overwhelming as they did before. Exercise also has the benefit of making you feel more energised and positive, and in that state of mind you are better able to combat those overwhelming feelings.

- *ACTION – create an exercise program – nothing complicated – just a list of exercises that you can do every day. You don't need expensive gym membership or complicated equipment: sit-ups, push-ups, step-ups – there are many effective exercises that you can do simply and cheaply.*

# Drugs & Alcohol

*NOTE: this section has some general and basic advice regarding drug and alcohol use. If you are struggling with these substances, or you know someone who is, you (or they) need professional help. Do not hesitate to contact a person or organisation for help – there are many available.*

Drugs and alcohol seem like a strange thing to be discussing in a book about being successful in high school but the unfortunate truth is that school is often when a person's involvement in these dreadful substances begins. I call them dreadful substances because nothing destroys lives more than drugs and alcohol. I will talk about 'drugs and alcohol' as if they are separate substances, but they are not – alcohol is as much a drug as heroine (and actually does more damage globally). The difference is that alcohol is legal in most places (at least for older people), but I still want to emphasise the danger that alcohol is to you and your success!

The reason that drugs and alcohol are such a danger to you and your success is that they can destroy everything that we have been talking about up to now. They can destroy your ability to think positively, kill your motivation, ravage your body, murder your sleep, and make it almost impossible to control your emotions – not a good recipe for success! You might think that I'm getting a bit carried away but I'm not the only one – look at the amount of money that governments around the world spend on preventing illegal drugs from getting over their borders, and the amount of money that goes into cleaning up the effects of legal drugs (such as alcohol and tobacco). It's literally billions and billions of dollars!

Drugs (especially alcohol) are linked to a huge amount of pain, suffering and loss throughout the world and people who get involved in them are asking for trouble. If you are looking for a key to success, drugs and alcohol are the furthest from it! Of course, there are successful people who take drugs and drink alcohol, and many of them will tell you that it has no impact on their success, but they are unfortunately deluded – maybe it's not noticeable, or they have not seen the impact, but they would be more successful and happier without drugs and alcohol. We can also examine the many lives which have been lost or destroyed through drugs and alcohol – famous actors, musicians, artists, writers, and ordinary people from all over the world can testify to the damaging impact of these poisonous substances.

The bottom line is – if you want to be successful you should avoid drugs in all their forms – including alcohol. You might agree that illegal drugs are bad but argue that a little drink every now and then is not going to hurt you. The reality is that so called 'soft' drugs often lead to 'hard' drugs and even a bit of 'poison' is doing you harm, even if you don't feel it. Add to that the risk of addiction (which studies have shown more than 10% of the population is prone towards) and even a small taste or try is too much of a risk.

So why are drugs so bad? A lot of study has been done on the impact of drugs (legal and illegal) on people. Occasionally you may hear of a single benefit of drugs in the news (it relaxes you, it strengthens your heart, etc.) but the problems outweigh any benefits more than 100 to 1. Let's examine some of the issues that drugs can cause.

## Impact on Relationships

When you take drugs (including alcohol) the chance of issues in your relationships increases. Studies have shown that those who regularly take drugs/drink have more relationship issues and broken relationships than those who don't. Taking drugs/alcohol doesn't mean that you are going to start fighting with everyone, but the risk increases – and it's not hard to see why when you look at all the emotional and physical effects that drugs have.

## Personal Safety

Drug affected people are more likely to be involved in traffic accidents, workplace accidents and general accidents around the home, and many of the people admitted to emergency departments are there because of the impacts of drugs. Add to this the safety risks of people from drug-related violence and the issue multiplies. Does that mean that if you get involved in drugs you are putting the safety of yourself and others at risk? Not immediately, but eventually, yes! The statistics are very clear.

## Loss of Concentration

Being able to concentrate is an important part of achieving your success, isn't it? Well, that's one of the first things to go when you get involved in drugs. All drugs have an impact on brain chemistry (we talked about how important that is in the last section) and for many of them (such as marijuana) it is cumulative – meaning that the more drugs you take over time the more impact it has.

In most cases the person taking the drugs will not realise the impact that it is having on them but others can see the impact (have you ever seen a drunk person struggling to stand up but insisting that they are not drunk?). The regular use of drugs of any kind alters the chemistry of the brain, sometimes permanently, and with some drugs the only way to 'solve' the problem is to take more drugs – this leads to dependence, which we'll talk about in a moment.

As someone who is determined to be successful, not just in high school but hopefully beyond, the use of drugs should be something that doesn't interest you at all. Everything that we've looked at so far in this book is about making changes in your life that help you reach your best and keep you there. Drugs do the opposite and should be avoided at all costs!

## Costs

Speaking of costs, the cost of drugs should also be a deterrent for those focused on their success. These costs can be divided into two groups: the cost to buy drugs, and the costs of using drugs. We've already looked at the costs of using drugs – including damage to your mind, body and life and to society generally. The cost of buying drugs can be just as damaging to an individual.

Statistics from across the western world show that most crimes related to the theft of property are perpetrated to support a drug habit – people break into a house, steal the TV and microwave, sell it to a guy who buys stolen goods and use the money to buy drugs. It's a dark and pathetic situation that demonstrates how desperate these people are to support their habit. Of course, it doesn't start like that. At first, they have a job, can pay for the drugs they want and life seems wonderful. Then they lose their job because of their drug habit (remember, they can no longer concentrate like they used to) and suddenly they are borrowing money from friends and family to pay for drugs. Eventually they are evicted from their apartment because they can't pay the rent, they 'borrow' money from friends and family until they have no friends left and their family can no longer trust them. The next step is crime, all to keep getting that feeling that drugs give them!

By the way, if you think that this type of scenario only applies to 'hard' drugs like cocaine and heroin, don't be fooled! Alcohol can destroy lives in much the same way, and tobacco is not much better. Whichever way you look at it the costs of drugs are too high.

### Dependence or Addiction

A very real danger of drugs is the risk of dependence or addiction. Some drugs provide you with a 'high' (you feel great, confident, invincible and happy) for an amount of time, and it's this feeling that first hooks drug users and what they chase when they take drugs. The problem is that the feelings don't last for long and when they are gone the user 'crashes' into a deep depression-like state where they feel horrible, miserable and depressed. To get back to the high they take more drugs.

This soon leads to dependence (where they feel like they cannot live to their fullest potential without the artificial boost) and then to addiction (where they will do almost anything to get their next 'fix'). People who are addicted lose their interest in all other aspects of their life (family, friends, job, exercise, food, etc.) and can literally fall apart. Nobody thinks that it can happen to them but that's the insidious nature of drugs – it catches a person unawares and dulls their brain so that they cannot see the danger they are in.

## Stress, Anxiety and Paranoia

The changes in brain chemistry that we have already mentioned can have serious impacts upon a person's mental health and wellbeing. Dependence upon drugs, even if it's only a 'slight' dependence ("it helps me to relax") can lead to situations where dependence upon a drug causes increased levels of stress and anxiety when the need is not met.

In extreme cases individuals can be subject to complete mental breakdowns and reality fractures. I had a neighbour who was affected by the drugs he took – he heard voices in the roof of his house and suffered from high levels of paranoia. The situation culminated in him assaulting me, police raiding his house and him being arrested. Without the drugs, he was a nice guy, but they changed him and ruined his life.

## Psychosis and Depression

A common result of prolonged drug use is psychosis and depression. Psychosis is when a person loses touch with reality and has difficulty functioning in the world. Depression is when the simplest problem becomes a major obstacle and it seems like the whole world is trying to make things worse. When a user gets to this stage drug use often increases because it seems to be the only solution. Family and friends are usually little help because they have been alienated or lost.

People who suffer from these types of mental issues need help but often do not get it because they are still denying the problem or they are so focused on getting another 'hit'. The cycle often ends with the police becoming involved and the individual getting the help they need in prison – if they are lucky.

**Physical Damage**
The final impact of drugs is the physical damage that is causes. This impact is often hidden because it isn't highlighted until after death. Besides the negative impacts that drugs have on the brain there are a range of problems that are caused by drugs in the rest of the body. Drugs that are inhaled (tobacco, marijuana, hash, etc.) can cause serious problems with the mouth, throat and lungs of users – we weren't meant to breath in smoke! Drugs that are ingested, taken through the mouth or nose, (alcohol, cocaine, ice, etc.) can cause serious difficulties with the mouth, nose, throat, stomach, liver and kidneys – only good things should be eaten/drunk. Drugs that are injected (heroin, etc.) can cause serious issues with veins and the heart – the only

time something should go into your veins is when you are donating or receiving blood.

Added to these concerns numerous studies have shown that drugs (including the legal ones) have clear links to cancers of the organs mentioned above and others. Cancer is one of the biggest killers in our society but they are usually recorded as separate cancers. If the true causes were recorded you would find that the number one cause of deaths in our society is drugs and alcohol! So, I'll say it one more time – if you want to be successful keep far away from drugs of all types!

# Computers

We're talking about computers in the lifestyle part of this book because, whether we realise it or not, computers are a part of our lives, and how we integrate them into our lifestyles will help determine our success. Like any tool a computer can be used well or not, the key is to ensure that your use of computers is going to increase your chances of success, not reduce them.

### Time your Use

One of the first principles of effective computer use is to ensure that you manage your time using the computer wisely. I've always found computers to have an amazing ability to speed up time – whenever I use one I focus on a task (such as writing or playing a game) and four hours magically passes, even though it only felt like a few minutes. The problem with that is that if you don't manage your time when you are using a computer you will find your time disappearing too fast.

**Plan your Time**

When you are using a computer, it is best to plan your time and how you are going to use your tools before you start. We will be looking at timetables in more detail later but that is essentially what you need to be doing. Successful people do not do things by accident, things don't 'just happen' for them – they plan, they prepare and they succeed.

Before you begin working, determine what you are going to be doing and what your goals are, then choose how you will achieve those goals. This is where you 'choose' whether to use a computer or not, yes, I said choose – you should not automatically go to your computer when you start working, it should be something that you do because it is the best option. Believe it or not, sometimes using a computer is not your best option.

Activities that you should use a computer for:
- Doing a large amount of writing;
- Researching on the internet;

- Recording or listening to podcasts;
- Watching instructional videos;

Activities you should not use a computer for:
- Planning any form of writing;
- Reading (an e-reader may be an exception);
- Writing or revising notes;
- Brainstorming or working with ideas;

The reason that computers are not recommended for the above activities is that they require a flexibility which cannot yet be provided on a screen. You may disagree, but experience has taught me that sometimes it's better to work with a good old pen and paper.

### Take Regular Breaks

As mentioned previously, computers have an almost magical ability to make time disappear, so it is vital that you plan to take regular breaks when you are using one. When you are sitting without movement for long periods of time (as when you are using a computer) the body shuts down your muscles and blood flow deceases. Regular breaks provide the body with the movement that it needs to get your blood pumping again.

Another benefit of regular breaks is that they can clear the mind – when you have been focused on one task for too long your mind becomes less able to find and explore new ideas. A break to get a drink, go to the toilet or a quick walk around the house will give your brain a quick refresh and enable you to get back to your task with new momentum. Try it and you will see that planning regular breaks makes your work more effective.

One of the best ways to ensure that you take regular breaks is to keep a glass of water near you and drink while you work. Before too long you will need to go to the toilet. That is a good opportunity to get up, go to the toilet and refill your glass with water for the next session. Remember that anything besides water will not work as well.

- *ACTION – take a break right now!*

**Organise your Desktop**

Computers make it very easy for users to access a wide range of apps, files and documents without much trouble, but the problem with that is the potential distractions that can get in the way. Who hasn't been working on something only to be momentarily distracted by an email, message or notification, only to find that a few hours have gone by while you responded?

It is important that you organise your computer desktop (or start screen, or whatever you call it) to minimise these distractions. It is possible to turn off your notifications, close distracting apps or even keep your school-related work on a separate virtual screen/desktop. Whatever you do, make sure that when you want to work nothing will get in your way.

If you are tempted to answer that message, or respond to that email, just remember what your goals are and what you are trying to achieve. If you give in to the temptation you will be losing your momentum and wasting your valuable time. If your communications are important then schedule them during your regular breaks so that they do not distract you from your work. Keep to the time you have assigned for your breaks and then when you get back to work put your messages/email away.

### Back-up Often
One of the advantages of using a computer is that you can save your work and come back to it later without any issues. A disadvantage is that there is the potential that you can lose all of it with one digital mishap. I know what it is like to lose 15,000 words of a novel, and have been with colleagues when they have lost a week's worth of report comments. Frustrating, to say the least!

Since my initial word loss, I have become a strong believer in regular back-ups. A back-up is a redundant (or extra) copy of all your files that are kept in a safe place away from your computer. When I was younger this had to be done with floppy disks or digital tapes – slow and annoying – but now creating back-ups is so much quicker and easier.

With cloud storage (*Microsoft's* OneDrive, *Google's* Drive and *Apple's* iCloud are some examples) it is simple to have you work saved to the cloud for safety and easy access. If you haven't set-up a cloud account do so now – they are free. However, I would still recommend having a separate back-up that you do yourself at home. This can be done with a portable hard drive which is not expensive and can be kept somewhere away from your computer. The advantage of having a physical back-up is that if there is a problem with the cloud (no access or it's been hacked) you can still access your files.

- *ACTION – When was the last time you backed-up your computer? Do it now. If your back-ups are already organised use the time now to run a back-up, if you haven't organised a regular back-up do it now.*

# TV & Music

Television and music are such a big part of our lives now that it would be remiss of me not to talk about how they fit in with your success in high school. The uncomfortable truth is that they generally have no part in your success – if you want to be successful you will have to manage your viewing and listening habits carefully. That doesn't mean that you cannot watch your favourite shows on TV or listen to your favourite music, it just means that you will have to do it all intentionally and with an understanding of what is beneficial and what is not.

**The Problems with TV**

Television is an amazing invention which has remained basically unchanged in the last 60 years. What this means is that our society has evolved to accommodate this box into our lives. Numerous families build their lives around what's on the TV: it's the first thing that goes on in the morning; returning home from school is timed to catch the afternoon cartoons; dinner is ready in time for 'prime time'; and bed time is not until after the nightly movie is finished. People let the box control them instead of the other way around!

Despite its entertainment value, television has some fairly negative physiological impacts. Studies have shown that after a few minutes of watching TV a person's brain waves are actually altered – they move into a less aware state where high brain processes cease to function. In effect watching TV makes you 'stupid'! Scientists are as yet unaware if prolonged exposure to TV has long-term effects but it can be argued that time spent watching TV is not as productive as reading or doing something a little more constructive.

Another impact of TV on the brain that has been identified by scientists is the reduction of the attention span of TV watchers. Have you noticed that everything on TV happens quickly? Ads bombard you with information rapidly in sub-30 second blocks and programs are filled with a series of quick events and actions. Over the long term this has produced people who are used to their information in short 'sound bytes' and they have difficulty concentrating for long periods of time. The more TV they watch, the worse it gets. Obviously, if you want to succeed at high school you need to have a decent attention span.

Television can also produce individuals who cannot think deeply. TV programs are designed to fit into set timeslots: programs are usually 30 or 60 minutes (including ads). That means that within that 30/60 minute timeslot the hero/heroine must discover the problem, try to overcome the problem, almost fail, but finally succeed. Of course, that is a generalisation but the usual 'formula' is similar. That means that there is no time for an exploration of deeper issues that may be a part of the problem, or the human characteristics that may form part of the problem or solution – it's all very shallow and neat. This may be convenient for a studio and production company but it doesn't produce deep-thinking viewers. People who watch a lot of TV are losing the ability to think deeply about issues that they encounter in their lives – it's just easier to accept what they are told on the TV!

TV also creates a form of exhaustion in the brain which feels like tiredness but can have more lasting effects. Television programs are carefully designed to grab and keep a viewer's attention. This is done by creating a rapid sequence of shots that constantly change and, in a way, hypnotise the brain to keep watching. Added to this are a constant rhythm of sounds which prevent the brain from relaxing by keeping it in a state of constant focus. Normally the brain can 'switch off' when you are using it and go into a type of 'automatic pilot' but when you watch TV this does not happen and the brain can become fatigued from constant focus.

### TV as a Distraction

Besides the negative impacts that television can have on watchers there is another huge problem with TV when it comes to succeeding in high school – it can be a huge distraction. When the TV is turned on it produces two things: light and sound, both of which can get in the way of your brain's processes and the task at hand.

Therefore, I recommend that students do not attempt to read or study in the same room as the TV. When you are in the same room as the TV your mind is torn between the task you are trying to achieve and the sights and sounds that it is being bombarded with every second. Even if the sound is turned off your brain is still attracted to the rapidly flashing light that emanates from the TV – your brain cannot help it, like a moth to a light or a baby to a flashing toy – it's irresistible!

If you try to work in another room but can still hear the TV you will have the same problem. The distraction might even be harder to resist because you can't look away from the sound. Every conversation, sound effect and piece of music that comes out of the TV will prevent you from focusing completely on your work. If you can complete it the finished product will not be your best.

The solution is to turn off the TV while you are working. A clearly established and consistent 'quiet time' for study may help other family members to respect your desire to get work done effectively. If everyone in the family knows that the hours between 4 and 6pm, for example, are time for you to get your work done without the TV, then it will be easier for everyone to co-operate. If you are unable to avoid working while the TV is on you could go somewhere quiet, like a neighbour's house or local library, or you could try using noise-cancelling headphones or just normal headphones with less distracting sound to cover the distraction of the TV.

## The Problems with Music

I know that I am about to tread on 'holy ground'! Music is sacred to many people and to stop them listening to their favourite music is like amputating an arm – it's painful and they can't function without it! But relax, I am not going to tell you what music you can or cannot listen to – you're old enough to make that decision, but I am going to get you to think about the music you listen to, why you listen to it and what effect it may be having on your success. Just like with everything else we've looked at – you shouldn't listen to music just because you always have or all your friends do.

Although there are many different genres of music in the world there are, in reality, only two types when it comes to young people like you: 'cool' music that you and your friends like, and everything else. Radio stations and cable music channels know this and will only ever play the 'cool' music – that is, music that is popular. That's fine, as far as entertainment goes but since the beginning of the 20th Century popular music has had distinctive characteristics: it is loud and it has beat/rhythm. That's not a bad thing for enjoyment but it's a killer for success in high school.

The loudness of modern popular music creates many issues. As we've already discussed in relation to TV, loud sound can be a major distraction when you are trying to get work done. Even worse, loud music interrupts your thinking patterns and prevents you from thinking about anything in depth. Think about what it was like if you've ever been to a live music concert – the band is beating out their tunes, the speakers are pumping, the crowd is going wild – much opportunity for thinking? Not really. That's the environment that any loud music creates, so it should be avoided when your focus is work.

Added to this issue is the obvious problem of the damage that high volume music can do to your hearing. Studies have shown that when modern young people reach their twenties a large portion of them have permanent hearing loss from listening to loud music. You may not think that losing a bit of hearing is a big deal but remember – once the ear is damaged it cannot be repaired – that damage is forever! Besides, for someone who is focused on their own success – how is losing a part of one of your senses going to contribute to your success? It always pays to turn down the volume a little, your future-self will thank you.

So, what music is okay for studying, you may ask? It depends on what you are doing. If you are doing something that requires no major brain power – like colouring-in a map or designing a cover for an assignment then listening to music is not going to get in the way, and it may even help you be more creative. However, if you are doing anything else which requires thought (including writing, reading, revising, planning, memorising, etc.) music will prevent you from doing your best. That includes music that is soft or gentle. This type of work is best done in silence, or near silence.

Remember that, despite what you may think, music does not help your brain work better – that myth (which we will discuss in more depth at the end of the book) comes from the idea that your brain can do many things at once. It's not true. Your brain can rapidly switch from one task to another but it can only focus on one thing at a time. That means when you are listening to music while you work your brain is constantly switching back and forth between your work and the music and it is not focused solely on your work – which is hopefully not what you want.

Now, I know what you are thinking. You are insisting that, despite the years of experience and numerous studies which clearly demonstrate that listening to music while studying is counter-productive, and that people cannot really multi-task, you are different from everyone else because you CAN listen to music while you study and it doesn't get in the way. In fact, you know that it makes you work better! You thought that, right? Well, I'm not going to argue with you. If you think that music enhances your thought processes – despite what science tells you – then you go ahead and listen to your music. But if you are honest with yourself you will know (deep down inside) that your work would be better and your success would be fuller if you gave your brain every opportunity to do its best.

## Online vs Offline

These days it is possible to find everything online. If you wanted to you could never leave the house and live your life through the Internet. Not very healthy, but possible. The reason we are talking about this is that the 'online reality' has become the place where young people spend much of their lives. They (you) play games online, interact with friends online, shop online, read, research and are entertained online. It's quick, convenient and easy – but is it the best way to exist? As someone who is interested in their success you need to examine your online presence and determine if it is the best way to achieve success in high school.

In all that we've talked about so far one of the key concepts I've tried to encourage is 'balance' – not doing too much of one thing. Even too much of a good thing is not good. When it comes to 'being online' young people lean towards 'too much' and that can become a problem.

### Disadvantages of Being Online
I don't think I need to spend any time telling you of the advantages of 'being online' but we probably do need to discuss some of the disadvantages:

- Being constantly online doesn't give you much opportunity for rest – when you are connected 24/7 there is not much time for you to stop, gather your thoughts, and just be still for a while (and we already know how important that is). I know of many students who are woken up by notifications throughout the night and then struggle to stay awake during class.

- Being online can be distracting – we have all experienced the times when we were busy working on something and a call/text/notification/email interrupted our train of thought. That one interruption can destroy an effective period of concentration. When this is happening constantly it is difficult to get effective work done.

- You have little control over the information – when notifications or texts or messages come to your device you have little control over what the information is. Yes, you can personalise your news service or social network feeds but you are still only a 'receiver' of the information. If you truly want to be successful you need to be a 'finder' or 'creator' of information.

- You can become dependent upon it – what would you do if all your devices suddenly stopped working and there were no replacements? If you are like most people these days you would go through some pretty serious withdrawal – almost like getting over a drug addiction! It is easy for us to become dependent upon our technology but it is rarely a good thing. Some scientists are even recommending regular time away from technology to prevent this type of dependence. The less dependent you are on it, the better.

- Being online restricts your access to other sources of information – earlier I mentioned the importance of balance in your life. One of the reasons for that is that if you are always relying on only one source for your information you risk losing your access if that source goes down (no electricity), and how can you trust the information you are receiving if it only ever comes from one source? Maps are a common example – these days everyone uses their phones to find places, but how many actually know how to use a physical map?

These are just a few ideas but they should be enough to give you pause – to think about your current habits. Are you spending too much time online? Would it be a good idea to spend less time 'hooked up' to all your friends, and their friends? Remember, how many of them are interested in your success?

It would also be a good idea to spend some time doing without your devices for short periods of time. A school in which I worked had regular trips organised for students to go 'out bush' – into the wilderness. They were not allowed to take mobile phones or other technologies and would spend a few days and nights without their usual online presence. At first it was difficult for the students, but after a while they accepted life without being connected and things started to change. The students would start talking to those around them more (sometimes with people they hadn't talked to before), they would become more aware of their surroundings, and suddenly feel a 'freedom' which many of them had never felt before. When they returned home they were more likely to think about their online presence and add a bit of balance to their lives – and they were always better for it.

If this concept sounds too difficult for you, or you find yourself making excuses for why it's not a good idea, it may mean that you are dependent upon being connected and that means it's even more important to separate yourself from these devices.

- *ACTION – try to create a time in your day when you are not connected. To start with it only needs to be a small amount of time (maybe an hour). Turn off all your devices for that time and enjoy the rest from the world. When the time is over get connected again – did you miss anything? Probably not. Try to increase the time spent 'disconnected' so that eventually a large part of each day is devoted to you and your goals, not your social network.*

## Community Involvement

Community involvement is you being more involved in your community. It may include being a member of sports or other recreational clubs, being involved in church or church-related activities, charities, adventure clubs, academic clubs, local art groups and regular involvement in local events, such as fairs. Being involved in some of these activities on a regular basis would require more time and energy and may seem like a bad idea when you are trying to succeed at high school, but that may not actually be the case.

**People who Do More, Do More**

The expression, "people who do more, do more" simply means that those people who have a busy schedule and are involved in a variety of activities generally achieve more with their lives than others who don't have any extra commitments. This may seem like a contradiction – the more you do, the more you can do, but follow the logic of it before you dismiss it. Someone who has extra commitments is usually more energised, more organised and more empowered to get things done. Their range of activities give them confidence and helps them develop competence in a variety of circumstances. This, in turn, gives them more confidence, greater competence, and so on in an upward spiral. These are the people whom others look at in admiration and ask, "where do you get the time to do all this stuff?!"

Of course, it is important to remember the principal of 'balance'. Someone who takes on too many extra activities and commitments is going to either fail to meet some of their commitments or have a major breakdown because they are doing too much. It's important to know what your limitations are and work within them. If you do not know what your limitations are it is best to start with only one extra commitment. For example, if you are becoming involved in church, continue with that for a while (say six months) before you join the local tennis club. When you have settled into juggling those two commitments, along with your school work you may find that you've reached your limit – that is, you can do no more. If that's the case, you can settle back and do your best in your new endeavours and enjoy the benefits that come from them. If you find that you haven't reached your limit then add another activity until you do. Just remember to take it very slow. It's better to add these commitments gradually than to add them quickly, but then having to drop one because it's too much.

## Build Networks

One of the advantages of community involvement is the networks that you can build. People who run successful businesses know the importance of networking and even have special network meetings just so that they can meet other people in their industry. Networks are important because you meet people who can help you, and whom you can help – helping people is a great way to build relationships.

As someone who wants to succeed at high school you will need plenty of help and creating networks provides you with opportunities to find the right people. You will find that the networks you build will be helpful long after you've finished high school. You will also find that the skills needed to meet people and develop networks will help you build confidence and familiarise yourself with how to work effectively with a variety of people.

How do you create a network? Find organisations that centre on activities or skills that interest you or areas in which you want to achieve; begin attending their meetings or become a member; spend time with people who have the skills you want or are involved in the activities you want to be involved in. Examples include: public speaking groups, gardening clubs, sports clubs and hobby or special interest groups. Meeting and spending time with these people will help you create networks that can last for your lifetime.

*NOTE: When you become more involved in your community there is a requirement that you spend more time with adults – this is usually a good thing but it does come with some risks. Ensure that you are never alone with an adult, and never give your personal details to someone you don't know. If possible, attend these meetings with a friend or two.*

## Develop Experience

The other major advantage of becoming involved in community activities is the experience that you gain. As a student, you are primarily involved in what you do at school (classes, lunch times with friends, maybe a sport or two, etc.) and at home (TV, music, friends, maybe chores, etc.) and there's not much else. Adding extra activities and commitments to your week adds a whole new dimension to your levels of experience. You will be involved in activities and events that most of your peers will not, you will go to places your peers haven't visited, and you will meet people that your peers never will. All of this will enhance your life experience and give you advantages well above that of the other students in your class, and even school!

Remember that the skills you learn in these extra activities (such as public speaking, writing, organisation, leadership, etc.) can carry over into your school work and beyond. Employers love to hire people who have a breadth of experience – it's not just about the grades! You will find that your extra experiences will make you more suited to success and more able to make use of it.

- *ACTION – create a list of clubs, associations or organisations that you would be interested in joining. If you are not aware of any do some research to discover which ones are active in your area. Contact them to find out more about them.*

## Family

*NOTE: this section offers some advice about family support. The advice is general and should not replace professional support. If you are part of a family in which any form of abuse is occurring you must seek help from other adults. Talk to your teachers or contact an organisation which can help you.*

Talking about family can be a risky proposition – many families are quite dysfunctional and the ideal is rarely a reality. But family can be supportive of you, even if it is dysfunctional. Your family should be a place of peace and support in your busy, pressured life and your home should be the place where you can retreat when life becomes too much – like a harbour in a storm. We'll be talking about how you can make the best use of your family to help you achieve your success.

If your family is not supportive, if they get in your way rather than helping you, if your home is not a peaceful and safe place to be – I am sorry. It is an obstacle – but it cannot be something that you should let stop you from achieving your goal of being successful at high school. There are many successful people who have achieved great things even though they came from uncaring or abusive homes. If you come from one of those homes you need to resolve to go on despite the difficulties – we'll briefly talk about what you may be able to do at the end of this section.

For most teenagers (if not all) home feels like a battleground. Parents seem like Public Enemy Number One and siblings are annoying at best. This is due to two main factors: Firstly, adolescence is a time when you begin finding and forming your own identity – answering the question: Who am I? Secondly, it's a time when you are being bombarded by hormones as your body puts your journey to adulthood into high gear. Both factors mean that home is sometimes the last place you feel at peace and your parents are the last people in which you feel like confiding.

Let me tell you (with lots of experience with both my own and many other adolescent lives) that these feelings are normal and are usually more about you than them. These feelings of rebellion are one way of finding your independence. That said, it is important for your success that you get past these feelings and focus on your success. You being successful is also important to your parents, so try to cut them some slack and let them help you when they can – it will make them feel a part of your life (which is very important to them) and it will give you some of the help you need. Remember that with your family supporting you, success will be much easier.

## Support
Remember how we talked about the importance of a support team to help you be successful – your family should be the closest part of your team. Whether you believe it or not your family knows you and wants to support you, and you should let them. Let them know that you are organised and have a program already in place (or that you are developing one with the help of this book) and that they can help you in several ways.

Your family can be supportive by just being there, by being someone to talk to or a shoulder to cry on, by co-operating with your study program, and by providing opportunities to help you reach your goals. There will be specific ways that your family can help you and it's important to think about these now so that you can discuss them with your family. This will demonstrate that you are taking control of your own learning and that will build their confidence in you.

Probably the easiest way that your family can help you (especially your siblings) is by giving you space to get your work done, by keeping quiet when you are trying to work and by motivating you to stick to your study schedule. There are many other ways but it's a conversation that you need to have with your family.

### Assistance

Most parents love helping their kids. In fact, many provide too much assistance and end up doing the work for them. I've seen it many times – students submit assignments that are just too good compared with their other work and I know that much of the work was done by Mum or Dad. The problem with that is that if you allow your parents to do the work you will not learn what you should have learned by doing the work yourself. Remember, learning is not just about the information, it's also about the processes involved and if you aren't involved in the process you won't get better at it.

So, what do you do about parents who want to help you too much? Firstly, be grateful that they are willing to help – it shows that they are interested in you, and that's a good thing. Secondly, do some of the preparation beforehand so that when you are sitting down with either Mum or Dad they can see that you've started the process and need just a bit of guidance. Thirdly, let them know that you are happy for their assistance with this assignment but that you need to do the work yourself – accept their advice, their input and their ideas but do the work yourself.

In most cases your parents will be glad that you are taking responsibility for your own learning and that you are happy for them to help. If they are not, they may just need some time to get used to the idea that their 'little baby' is growing up.

### Non-Supportive Families

If you happen to live in a family that is not supportive (maybe because your parents are working too hard to help you, they are not there, or any number of other reasons) there are a few things that you can do. Firstly, remember that you are the one who is ultimately responsible for your own success so you should not use a lack of family support as an excuse to fail. This is just another obstacle that you must overcome, and you can do it. It may be harder for you than for other students who have family support but rather than stopping you that should make you more determined.

If you find no support at home you can try looking elsewhere: do you have other relatives (uncles, cousins, etc.) who would be willing to assist you? Are you able to find help at local libraries or other community groups? Are you able to seek help with members of your local church? Does your school offer after school study groups with teachers in attendance? (If not, why not start one up?) What about going to a friend's house and 'sharing' their parents? The point is, try your hardest to find a solution so that you can still be successful. And remember that a dysfunctional family is not your fault.

## A Rest Day

The idea of a rest day is very old. It was first mentioned at the very beginning of the Bible – after God created the world he rested. Not because he needed to rest but because he knew we would need to rest and he set the example for us. Since that time, a day of rest has been observed primarily for religious reasons but there are good (non-religious) reasons for having a weekly rest day.

Much research has been done into the benefits of having a 'sabbath' (the Hebrew word for 'rest') each week. The benefits include physical rest, reduced stress, clarity of mind, improved relationships, improved happiness and even a longer life. Even high-profile corporate and motivational speakers extol the advantages of having a day of rest each week.

In fact, there are many people who are responsible for multi-million dollar empires who manage to take regular time each week away from their busy schedule to rest. During that time, usually a day, they don't answer their business phone, check their email or do any work at all. And instead of being a day behind when they return to work, they are more productive than if they didn't rest.

Some of these very successful people have 'total' rest days – that is, they don't work or do things that they normally would during the week – it's a total day off. Others have 'partial' rest days – that is, they rest from their phone, or email, or the TV or the computer, technology in general or whatever it is that can distract them. The day that they gain is used to spend time with family (meals, exercise and activities together) and themselves (solitude, meditation/prayer, reading, etc.).

At the end of their rest day they are well-rested, recharged and ready for the new week.

The evidence speaks for itself – a rest day is an important ingredient of success. It may sound counter-productive but taking a day off each week makes you more productive and effective. Obviously when and how you take the day off is an individual thing – what works well for one person may not for someone else. So, it's all about experimenting with what works best for you.

- *ACTION – choose a day that will become your 'sabbath' (because of school it will probably have to be on the weekend). On that day consciously take a break from the usual school work you would be doing, including technology. Put it out of your mind and focus on the other aspects of your life (family, friends and self). To avoid excess guilt you may, at first, need to work extra hard on the other day of the weekend but eventually your well-rested self will work more efficiently on the other six days and you can enjoy your guilt-free rest.*

# Lifestyle Action Plan

1. Assess your current diet, exercise regime and sleep habits — are they going to help you be your best? Consider what can you do to improve what you eat, how you exercise and how long you sleep?

2. Are you in control of your emotions? Reflect on what can you do — today — to improve your emotional well-being.

3. Determine right now to be purposeful in the use of your electronic devices. Kick the habit of automatically switching them on and instead consciously control your use of them.

4. Think about how you can become more involved in your community — take steps to that end before the end of the week.

5. Take a moment (right now) to tell each member of your immediate family that you want to be successful and that you really want them to be a part of your success.

6. Choose one day of the week that can be your 'rest day'. Decide to reserve that day for yourself and family instead of work and distractions.

# Part 3 – Goals

*Goals determine what you're going to be.*

*Julius Erving*

Goals are one of the most important strategies for finding success. Every person who is successful in their field (whether it's business, sport, politics, art or any other area) has used goals to guide them towards success. A goal is like a map to the treasure – if you don't have the map you can dig holes all over the place but your chances of finding the exact spot where the treasure is buried is almost zero! With a map, you can find where the treasure is buried and start digging – it's still going to take much work but your success is almost guaranteed.

Everyone knows about goals. Everyone talks about them. Some people even stick them up on their walls, but few people spend enough time thinking about, developing and organising their goals. Unless this is done in a systematic way your goals will not be as effective as they can be. Ineffective goals are better than none, but effective and motivating goals are going to make your success a reality sooner and much more powerfully. Let's spend some time looking at how to make these types of goals.

## Write it Down

One of the most important things that you need to do with your goals is write them down. In fact, goals that are not written down are not even goals – they are wishes or dreams, and they will not contribute to your success. Writing down your goals gives them power and makes them more real to your subconscious mind. That gives them an 'energy' which increases your chance of reaching them.

You can write them down on a small scrap of paper which is then left in the bottom of your sock drawer, but I would recommend writing them large and sticking them on the wall. This way you can see them all the time – they will be reinforced each time you look at them. Even better, share them with family and friends, stick them on the fridge or post them online and get the whole family involved in keeping you accountable to your goals.

## The Two Ps of Goal-Making

There are two characteristics of goals which will make them more powerful: they must be written in the present tense; and they must be personal. When your goals include these two characteristics they will be easier to build towards each day.

### Present Tense

Writing your goals in present tense means that you write them as if they have already been achieved, not in the future. For example, "I **have** received a grade of 95% on my History Assignment" rather than "I **will** receive a grade of 95% on my History Assignment." Notice the difference – when you write your goals in present tense they will appear as if they have already been completed to your subconscious mind and will then seem more real. This also paints the goal in a positive way – you've already achieved it and it feels good!

### Personal

Making your goals personal means that you will state them using "I", as in "I have won the writing Prize in English". When you write your goals in this way you personalise them and make them yours. Your subconscious mind will 'own' them and work harder to help you achieve them. It also helps when you speak these personalised goals out loud – it sounds like you are making a statement of fact, further reinforcing the goals in your mind.

# SMART Goals

For your goals to be effective they must be smart. The principle of SMART goals was developed from the acronym S.M.A.R.T which represents Specific, Measurable, Achievable, Results-focused and Time-based. This is a system used by successful people to develop goals which are more effective. Let's examine each component:

**Specific**

Effective goals are specific, rather than general. To create a specific goal, you must focus on what you want in a lot of detail – that helps to clarify the goal to your subconscious, makes the goal more real to you and gives you something clear to aim for. A specific goal has a lot of detail. It's more than just a wish or an idea. For example, a general goal could be "I have passed the final exam." To make that goal more specific you would say "I have achieved a grade of 96% in my final English exam." It's that detailed! When your goal is that specific you will work towards it with more focus and have a better chance of achieving it than a general goal which has no detail.

**Measurable**

Effective goals are measurable, that means that they can be easily measured and it's easy to identify when the goal has been achieved. If a goal is not measurable it's going to be hard to know when you have achieved it. For example, a goal which is not measurable would be "I have done well in English this year." How will you know if you have done 'well'? To make it measurable you would say "I have achieved a grade of B+ or better in English this year." With this goal, you will know you have achieved it when you get a grade of B+ or better.

## Achievable

An achievable goal is one that can realistically be reached by you with a bit of effort – it must be realistic. It is important to ensure that your goals challenge you (that is, it makes you do more than you normally would) but that it is not so far beyond your abilities that you have no chance of reaching it. For example, a goal which is not achievable would be "I am at the top of the class in French," if you have never learned French before. An achievable goal must consider your skills, knowledge and abilities and then stretch them a little bit.

## Results-Focused

It is important to make your goals results-focused. That means they will be aimed at what you achieve, not what you do. For example, a goal that is not results-focused would be "I will study hard every night." Although this would be a good thing to do it is not an achievement, as such. Your achievements should be something definite that you can work towards, like a specific grade in a specific subject.

**Time-Based**

Effective goals are time-based. That means they can be set within a time frame of days, weeks, months or years. With a deadline, your goal will seem more urgent and you will feel more motivated to work towards it. For example, a goal which is not time-based would be "I have become the First Speaker for the school Debating Team." A noble achievement but when will you have achieved it? By the end of next week? Next year? A time-based goal would be "I have become the First Speaker for the school Debating Team by the end of the year."

# Results or Process Goals

Another way to look at goals is by dividing them into either results or outcomes-based goals and process or activity-based goals. These two types of goals focus on a different part of your success and can be used to achieve different things.

**Results or Outcome-based Goals**

Goals focused on your results or outcomes are best when you are familiar with the processes involved in achieving the results you desire, that is, you know what to do – then you can focus on the results of your actions. For example, a results or outcome-based goal would be "I won the Public Speaking Award for my level at Graduation this year." You know how to do it and you just need to focus on achieving the result.

**Process or Activity-based Goals**
Goals focused on the process or activity are best when you are still developing the process which will help you achieve success. This is when you focus more on what you are doing and less on what you hope to achieve – that usually comes later. An example would be when you are learning to ride a bike your goal could be that you will practise riding for an hour each night, until you become proficient, then you can develop goals based on results.

# Breaking Goals Down

A final principle that is important to remember when developing goals is to break them down into smaller components. Larger goals will generally seem overwhelming because of their size but if you break them down into smaller components they will become more manageable. It's the same with long term goals – they are too far away and too indistinct to be motivating, but if they are broken down into months or weeks they will become more manageable.

**Large Goals**

A goal that is too large can be counter-productive – it's like trying to shove a whole burger into your mouth, you're more likely to choke on it. But if you take smaller bites you can finish off the biggest burger without too much effort. When you are confronted with a large goal try thinking about how to break it into smaller parts: there may be separate sections that you can focus on individually; or there may be a series of steps that you can follow.

For example, a goal of "I have achieved a grade of 97% for the Major Science Project" is too large. Something like a major project has many different parts and involves a complicated process to complete, but if it's broken down into smaller parts it will be easier to monitor and achieve. An example of how this could be done is below:

- I have chosen a topic for the Major Science Project by the end of Term One (T1).
- I have read three books on the topic by the end of Week 3, T2.
- I have interviewed Professors Jones and Chan at the University by the end of Week 6, T2.

- I have completed the first draft of the project by the end of Week 1, T3.
- I have completed the second draft of the project by the end of Week 3, T3.
- I have had three adults check the project for me by the end of Week 8, T3.
- I have completed the Final draft of the Project by the end of T3.

This example shows that the large goal can easily be broken down into smaller steps that can be measured and achieved over the life of the task. This means that every step of the way you will be able to know if you are on target or behind, and there will be less chance that you will get lost or confused during the process.

### Long-Term Goals

A goal that is too far away can 'get lost' in the busyness of a typical school year, that's why it's vital that long-term goals are broken down into shorter-term goals that can be followed and monitored without their getting lost. A very distant long-term goal might be "I have graduated from high school in 2023," which can easily be broken down into yearly goals leading up to the main one, such as "I have finished in the top 20% of my Year 7 class in 2018;" "I have finished in the top 15% of my Year 8 class in 2019;" and so on. This will give you something more manageable to work towards each year and improve your chance of achieving the larger goal.

Long-term goals can also be broken down into smaller time periods, such as yearly goals broken down into monthly, weekly and even daily goals. An example of this is as follows:

- I have achieved a grade of 95% for my final Science exam.

This can be broken down into monthly goals like this:

- I have started a science study group with friends by the beginning of April.
- I have created study notes for the first chapter of the Science textbook by the end of April.

These can be broken down even further into daily goals like this:

- I have reviewed the science study notes before dinner.
- I have responded to the emails from the rest of the study group before going to bed.

I hope you get the idea. The trick is to turn your long-term goal into a series of bite-sized, easy to follow goals that will make achieving the bigger one easier.

# Prioritising Goals

Having goals and working towards them is vital for success but it is not the end of the process. When you have many goals, it is possible to spend time focused on less important goals at the expense of more important ones. We tend to focus on urgent tasks rather than important ones but it is vital to know the difference. A task that is urgent is one that should be done soon but there wouldn't be serious consequences if it is not done. A task that is important may not be due soon but there are serious consequences if it is not done. An example of an urgent task is a minor pop quiz in Science tomorrow – it would be good to study for it but not at the expense of a major test in Geography next month, that's an important task, but is less urgent. Failing the pop quiz would have minor consequences but failing the major test could be serious. Therefore, it's important to recognise which of your tasks are urgent and which are important, and then prioritise your goals accordingly.

The way to prioritise your goals is to ask yourself which one of your goals would cause the greatest consequences if it were not completed – that is your highest priority goal. That is the task that you should focus on. This doesn't mean that you will ignore all other tasks – you must continue to work on those, they just will not be your main priority.

It is also important that you take deadlines into account when considering your most important goals. For example, if you have a very important task that is not due for a couple of months but a less important one is due next week you should prioritise the task due next week, even though it is less important. This is when you need to balance the urgency and importance of your goals. Consider the following graphic:

| 1<br>IMPORTANT<br>URGENT | 2<br>IMPORTANT<br>LESS URGENT |
|---|---|
| 3<br>LESS IMPORTANT<br>URGENT | 4<br>LESS IMPORTANT<br>LESS URGENT |

This demonstrates the logic behind choosing which goals to prioritise over others. Goals that are important and urgent (due next week) should be highest on your priority list. Goals that are important but less urgent should be next on your list. You can focus on the less important goals in the time you have remaining after the important goals have been dealt with.

So, what does this mean in practical terms? Soon after classes begin it will seem like you have too many tasks and not enough time to complete them all – this is when developing and prioritising your goals in vital. Place all your goals into one of the above categories – Important/Urgent (1), Important/Less Urgent (2), Less Important/Urgent (3), Less Important/ Less Urgent (4). The number represent the importance of the goals: 1 is more important than 2, etc. Then list all your goals in order of importance: 1s first, 2s second, and so on. Now all your goals are prioritised. Each night you should plan to focus first on the Group 1 goals, then Group 2 goals, and so on. This will ensure that the important goals are achieved, but not at the expense of the less important ones.

## Goals Action Plan

1. Create a space on one of the walls in the place where you study to place all your major goals – make it a habit to read through them every day.
2. Write out the Acronym S.M.A.R.T. and what each letter represents. Now place it somewhere near your study space and look at it every day to remind you of how your goals should be constructed.

3. Choose one long term goal in each of the following areas: school, relationships, and health, and make them a special focus for the rest of the year.

# Part 4 – Habits

*Successful people are simply those with successful habits.*

*Brian Tracy*

One of the best ways to ensure that you are successful in high school is to adopt or develop positive habits. Habits are actions that we do without thinking, like scratching your nose or brushing back your hair – you do it so often that it becomes a part of who you are. Most of the time you are not even aware that you are doing it. By developing certain habits, you will make doing the things that bring you success a part of your life. Let's look at the activities that you should develop into habits.

## Regular Progress Reviews

A progress review involves taking some time to look at where you are and what you are doing, and think about how you can improve your situation. Most people go through life from moment to moment, and most students go through their education from class to class without taking time to examine how they are performing and how they can improve. By reviewing your progress, you will separate yourself from the crowd and begin the exciting journey towards constant improvement.

Reviews should be conducted with a pen and paper in hand. Jot down questions and answers, thoughts and ideas, problems and solutions, and goals. If you fail to write it down it will soon fade and the process will not be helpful. If you do write it down the ideas will solidify and clarify in your mind and you will find your goals being achieved quicker than you thought possible!

Progress reviews should be completed on a regular basis and can be divided into four time periods: yearly, termly, weekly and daily. This provides insight into your progress throughout the entire year and helps you monitor your short and long-term goals. Let's look at each of these in turn.

*Note: it is important during these reviews that you focus only on those things that you can change – over which you have control. For example, wanting to make your younger brother more agreeable is pointless because you don't control your brother – what you can do is change the way you respond to your brother because that's something you can control.*

## Yearly Reviews

Most people conduct a yearly review without knowing it – they call it a 'New Year's resolution'! Think about it, to adopt a New Year's resolution, you must first have an idea about what needs to be improved in your life. The problem is that most people don't put a lot of thought into it and then they don't review their resolution on a regular basis.

To conduct an effective yearly (or annual) review you must set some time aside when you can reflect and think about your life and work over the past year. This cannot be done in front of the TV or when you are with friends – it must be done during a time of solitude when there are no interruptions.

Reflect on all the aspects of your life: relationships, school, physical fitness and health, personal growth, spiritual, financial, etc. In each of these categories think about what is going well, and what is not, then think about how you can improve. For example, in relationships you may want to argue with your parents less, at school you may want to improve your grades, in fitness and health you may want to lose weight, and so on.

You may come up with many areas in which you can improve but it is important not to overwhelm yourself –

a couple of items in each area is enough. It is better to improve a little each year than to start off with big plans but fail because you have too much to do! Once you have your areas for improvement you must write them down – these will become your goals for the year. Refer to the last section if you can't remember how to write your goals. Now you must ensure that you monitor your new goals.

- *ACTION – in each of the categories of your life (those listed above) make a list of each of the areas in which you think you can improve. Prioritise the list according to how important these are to you. Use this list to create your regular progress reviews.*

**Termly Reviews**
Conduct a review of your progress at the end of each school term – this is usually about 2 ½ to 3 months. Completing a review more than once a year is important because without a review it's difficult to know if you are on target, and if you are not on target it's too late to change if the year has already passed.

To review your progress throughout the term simply do what you did for the annual review but just for the one term – find a quiet place and time and ask yourself how you have gone in each of the areas that you have chosen to make your goals. Have you been working towards your larger, yearly goals? Have you overcome any problems that you faced? Do you need to modify your goal because it's too unrealistic or badly timed?

Sometimes you may find that you are a long way from achieving one or more of your goals and you have made only a little progress towards it. Analyse your progress – is there anything you could have done better, or differently? If there is, then change your approach so that your progress improves for the next term. If there isn't anything you could have done better then maybe you need to modify your goal. That's okay – success is not about being perfect, it's about constantly improving and getting better. Remember, goals are not written in stone – they can be modified to suit you and your circumstances.

### Weekly Reviews

To better achieve the goals that were identified during your termly review you need to review your progress on a weekly basis. This doesn't have to be a lengthy process but you will find that the time you invest into weekly and daily reviews will be paid back to you as increased effectiveness and efficiency.

Weekly reviews are best at the end of the week when your mind is still fresh from the activities and events that have happened. Don't wait until Sunday night to review the past week – it's too late and you should already be focused on the coming week. On Friday afternoon, straight after school, find a quiet place and go through the events of the week. How much time have you put into working towards your goals? Are you happy with how the week has gone? Why, or why not? What changes can be made to improve the next week?

You will find that when you start the week after having reviewed the previous week you will have more control of what happens, you will be more confident and things will seem easier. Suddenly, you will be progressing through life on purpose, having thought through things and prepared yourself for eventualities. You will be amazed at how these regular reviews change you and your life.

**Daily Reviews**
The final, and most important step, in regular reviews is the daily review. The daily review keeps you on target and 'fine tunes' your progress. Imagine you are travelling to a place you've never been – wouldn't it be better to check the map often to ensure that you don't lose your way? That's what daily reviews are.

Daily reviews are best done at the end of each day, just before you settle down for sleep. Think about the day, what happened, what went well and what didn't. Think about how the day could have gone better, and think about what you could have done to make the day more successful. Remember, this is not about reliving bad experiences but learning from them – that way you will reduce their occurrence in the future.

Once you have reviewed the day write down your thoughts and your conclusions – this will become your plan for tomorrow. We'll talk more about this when we look at lists, next. Keep in mind (or view) what your short and long-term goals are so that when you make your plan you can focus on these. That will ensure that your goals are not forgotten in the bustle and busyness of life.

If you regularly review your progress (years, terms, weeks and days) you will find that you become more organised and achieve more, you will find that life has become less stressful and that your grades continually improve – all for the cost of a few minutes each day. It looks like a good exchange to me!

*NOTE: some people find that using a template makes the process of reviewing your progress easier. If that's you, you may want to try using the review template that I've included with the resources at the end of this book.*

## Lists

Lists are one of the best ways to organise yourself and a vital step in being successful. Lists are sometimes looked at as being either a bit strange (only for crazy people) or something that's only useful when doing the grocery shopping, but nothing could be further from the truth! Many successful (and quite normal) people use lists to organise themselves, manage their goals, complete their tasks and stay motivated. They are a little-known weapon in the fight against failure. Let's look at how you can use lists to be more successful.

A list is quite simply a collection of ideas, tasks, goals, or anything else written vertically down the page. People have been using lists for millennia but they have not been considered important until recently. Although it's such a simple thing a list can be very powerful. It can turn a disorganised, unmotivated, stressed person into an ordered, energised and relaxed one.

The benefits of lists (in a list!) include:
- They are quick and easy to create,
- They can be created anywhere on any device,
- They can help you measure your progress,
- They can be modified easily,
- They can be shared easily,

- They can motivate you to complete your tasks/achieve your goals,

All of this from a few words on the page! The magic of lists is that they force you to think about your tasks/goals in an ordered way and keeps them ordered and organised each time you look at them. That's much more effective than the alternative – trying to think about what task you must complete next, and wondering if you have missed something.

The most common form of list is a To Do Lists – as the name suggests, it's a list of tasks or goals that you have set yourself to complete. To Do Lists can be used in a variety of circumstances, from a list of goals for the year to a list of daily tasks. They give you direction and help you stay focused on what needs to be done.

It is important to prioritise your To Do Lists, that means put the most important item first, second most important item second, etc. (We discussed this earlier). If you do this and then start from the top of your list you will be starting with the most important task or goal. This ensures that when you are working through your list you will be focusing on the most important thing, rather than spending valuable time on things that are less important. That means that if you run out of time, at least the most important items will have been completed.

Make sure that you check off items on your To Do List as they are completed. This will help you monitor your progress and keep you motivated. Interestingly, when a person checks off a completed task on their To Do List they receive a rush of natural 'happy chemicals' which make them feel good – like a natural high. This feeling keeps you motivated to continue achieving and helps you to form a habit of achievement – a sure way to succeed.

## Use a Planner and Wall Calendar

One of the best habits to develop is use of a planner and wall calendar. Planners (also called organisers or diaries) are books or applications which allow you to insert appointments and tasks on particular days in advance. Wall calendars are obviously calendars that you stick on your wall. Both are often supplied by schools or can be bought quite cheaply from office supply and stationery stores. Make it a priority to get both early.

Most people stumble from task to task without a clear idea of where they are going or how to get there. A planner and wall calendar will clarify to you what upcoming tasks you have and ensure that you can adequately plan for each one. This makes you proactive (you choose when to act) rather than reactive (you respond to the actions of others).

## Planners

Planners are vital for your success because they are the best way to organise yourself. Your planner should become an extension of your hand – carry it to every class, appointment and meeting – and write every assessment, task, project, meeting appointment and idea down in it. Doing this ensures that you will not forget important tasks and appointments. "But I have a great memory", you might argue. That may be the case, but are you certain that at the end of that Science class just before lunch – when your friends are telling you to hurry up, you are hungry, you remember that you have a note for your English teacher, you have a Student Council meeting at lunchtime, and your science teacher is rushing out the door – you can remember all the details of the Science Assignment you've just been given? Probably not! That's why you write those details down.

You planner is the place for task details (what to do) and due dates (when it needs to be done). These two pieces of information can save you a lot of time and worry and will help you to succeed in every task you attempt. Your average week contains multiple individual tasks and appointments and it is important to know what you have planned and when you are able to plan new activities or events. The successful business owner keeps track of their tasks and appointments in a similar way so this is a good habit to develop for later use.

There are also digital planners that you can buy, whether they are dedicated PDAs or apps for phones/tablets, but they are not a good alternative to paper-based systems (yet). Even if you are averse to using a paper-planner the benefits outweigh any problems: paper is instant – you don't need to turn on or wake up a device; paper is cheaper – if you lose your paper planner it may be inconvenient but will not cost a lot to replace; paper is more water resistant – wet paper is annoying but it still works when dry; paper doesn't need to be charged all the time; and finally, the physical act of writing things down on paper helps to clarify them in your mind and memory.

**Wall Calendars**

A wall calendar may seem a bit old fashioned in these days of 'digital everything' but it still has many benefits that technology usually can't match. The biggest advantage of a wall calendar is that it allows you to see the entire year in one glance and unless you have a screen the size of a wall at your house you won't get that with technology. The benefit of seeing the entire year is that you are better able to plan your work (and life) when you know what's coming up.

Let's look at an example: Gary's birthday is in April. If he didn't have a wall calendar he would not forget when his birthday was but he may not notice that three major assignments are due at around about the same time. Without a wall calendar those assignments may creep up on him and before he knows it he has lots of work to complete and a party on the same night. That's a recipe for disaster which can be avoided with a wall calendar.

Here's how to best use a wall calendar:

- First, find a place for it that is within sight and reach of where you work – this will enable you to see and access it regularly so that it becomes a part of your planning process;
- Second, enter all your personal events onto the calendar (birthdays, family trips, etc.) – don't worry about old Aunt Agatha's dinner party, only include events that you cannot miss or ignore (sorry Aunt Agatha!);
- Third, enter the term dates for the entire year including term breaks and all public holidays – it's good to know when you have classes and

when you don't, and when you will have more flexibility for study;

- Fourth, enter any school-related events (such as camps or excursions) that you are aware of, and add them as you become aware of them – these are those days when you will miss class and may not be able to keep to your regular study schedule. Knowing that will help you plan more effectively;

- Fifth, enter any assessment due dates that you are aware of and add them as you become aware of them – these are the 'nuts and bolts' of your success at high school. You cannot afford to miss them.

Once you have filled in all the information that is available to you, study that calendar for patterns. Ask yourself: are there any times when multiple assessments are due on or near the same day? Are there any days or weeks in which no or few assessments are due? Are smaller, less important (notice I didn't say 'unimportant') assessments due near more important ones? It's patterns like these that will help you plan your terms, weeks and days more effectively. By the way, remember that you must add or delete items as you become aware of them so that your calendar is always up to date.

# Avoid Procrastination

Procrastination is when you find reasons for not working on, or are easily distracted from, important tasks. It is one of your greatest enemies if you are trying to be successful and unfortunately it does not affect only students. Adults from across the globe, in a range of jobs and responsibilities struggle with procrastination. That is why it is important for you to develop the habit of avoiding procrastination. This will enable you to work productively, not just in high school, but beyond into university and your career.

Following are several suggestions that can help you reduce or eliminate procrastination. Use them as they are or modify them to fit your own way of doing things – just ensure that you get started!

- Identify the things that stop you from getting your work done. Is it the noise from the neighbours? Or a poster on the wall that you can't stop looking at? Maybe it's that friend who keeps sending messages. Or maybe it's just that you find the work too hard. Whatever it is: close it, move it, turn it off, or do whatever you need to do to change the situation. If you can reduce the obstacles you will get more done.

- Have goals that will motivate you to keep working. We talked about goals earlier and how having them will help you be focused and organised. Goals will also help you to avoid procrastinating by keeping your attention on your task. This is especially the case if you can have your goals within easy view so that you can check them off as you complete them.

- Set deadlines for all your tasks. Having a deadline helps you to stay focused and motivated to complete a task. Having a goal that is set by you (not the teacher) makes it stronger and more personal. That doesn't mean that you can choose when to hand in your assignments but that when the teacher gives you a due date you set your own deadline to complete the work before the teacher's due date.

- Reward yourself when you complete set tasks. It's human nature to want more of what we like, so if you link what you like with a task you will be more likely to complete that task. For example, if you set yourself an hour to complete a research paper for History and tell yourself that as a reward for completing the assignment you will play for favourite computer game, or chat with friends on the phone, or go for a run for 30 minutes you will be more motivated to complete the task. And, more importantly, if you continue to reward yourself in these ways you will develop the habit of getting your work done. Just be careful not to reward yourself with too many things that can do more harm than good, such as chocolate, ice cream, TV, etc.

- Plan and break down your tasks on paper. When you plan your task, and break it down into smaller, more manageable pieces you will find it easier to start and maintain your progress on the task. When the task seems too large and overwhelming you will be more likely to procrastinate on it, but if seems quite easy to manage you will get started and complete it. More on this later.

- Prepare all equipment you need before you start. There is nothing worse than concentrating hard on a task and then having to stop because you need something from another room. Your train of thought is lost and will take time to regain, and the trip to retrieve the forgotten item turns into a lengthy discussion with a family member. To avoid such interruptions, have all your equipment close before you start, then you can continue until it is finished.

- Do the easy bits first. When you start with parts of your task which are simple it is easier for you to get started on them – they don't seem overwhelming and it doesn't take effort to get started. Once you have started it is easier to maintain your momentum and keep going.

- Start with the hardest part. This is the opposite of the last point so you can try both and see which one works best for you. When you start with the hardest part of your task first you will get it over with – now the rest of the task will be easier. Finishing will not be difficult because you know that less energy is required for the easier elements of the task.

- Think about the bad consequences of not doing it. To motivate yourself you can think about the negative things that will happen if you do not complete the task. Bad grades? Failure? Damaged reputation? Disappointed family? To avoid these negative consequences, you will be more motivated to start and keep working.

- Think about the good consequences of doing it. Once again, an opposite suggestion. If you prefer dwelling on the positive, think about all the good things that will happen when you do complete the task. Better grades? Passing? Improved reputation? Proud family? Dwelling on these positive consequences will motivate you to get the job done so you can enjoy the benefits.

- Don't worry about perfection. Doing a good job is important and certainly something to aim for but sometimes perfection can be an excuse to procrastinate. 'If it's not perfect, why bother' is the attitude that can stop the most talented person from completing a task. Accept that it doesn't have to be perfect right from the start and get the job done. After it's completed you can spend time perfecting it.

So, you can see that there are many ways to avoid procrastination. Once you do these on a regular basis they will become a habit and you will find finishing tasks easier. Just remember that the fight with procrastination is a life-long battle that is never truly won – you'll struggle with it every day.

## Establish Routines

Routines are set ways of doing things that are repeated on a regular basis and they are an important part of success. If you develop positive routines you will find that achieving success becomes easier and you get more done. An example of a routine is coming home from school, grabbing a snack, going for a 30-minute run, reading for 30 minutes and then completing 45 minutes of study – and this is the same every day – a routine. You will find that once you have completed this routine on a regular basis it will become second nature to you and you won't even have to think much about it.

Let's look at the benefits of routines:

- Routines help you avoid distractions – one of the worst 'killers' of success are distractions – you start a task but remember something else and spend the next hour on a task that is less important. A routine will help you to stay focused on tasks that you know are going to contribute to your success.
- Routines help you think less but be more focused – if you could think less about what you need to do and what you are doing, and more about how you are doing it you would be more focused on your tasks and much more effective. Routines help you do this by making your tasks automatic.
- Routines make you more productive – by doing set tasks automatically each day you will find that you achieve more because you are distracted less. That means you will get more done and have more time to spare.

- Routines help you use less energy — the average person uses a lot of mental energy deciding what to do. When your tasks are automatic you can devote that energy to completing the task.

- Routines make it easier to act — often it is difficult to get started with a task, but when it is a part of a routine — something that you do regularly — you will find that getting started, and maintaining your momentum, is much easier.

- Routines reduce the pressure — we all know what it's like when a deadline sneaks up on you — you thought you had weeks left to finish that assignment, but suddenly it's due tomorrow! A routine will help you spread out your work so that a little bit is done each day and you're not leaving it until the last minute. It's much less stressful.

- Routines eliminate decision fatigue — decision fatigue is a term for what happens when someone who has been making too many decisions doesn't have the energy to make any more. Each decision we make takes mental energy, and we keep making decisions until eventually we tire and find decision-making difficult. Routines help to eliminate decision fatigue by making many of your usual decisions (such as 'Shall I work on my Geography homework now?") automatic.

- Routines reduce cognitive load – cognitive load is the term given to the energy you use to think about an activity. The more you must think about an activity the less energy you have for future activities – each person has a limited amount of energy each day and if you think about lots of activities you run out of energy and cannot think about any more. Routines help to reduce cognitive load by making regular decisions automatic so you don't have to think about them as much and you have energy for other things.

- Routines can take advantage of natural rhythms – everyone has natural rhythms, or times when they are more alert and times when they are less alert. For example, I struggle to keep my eyes open mid-afternoon but am wide awake late at night. By setting up your routines to take advantage of your natural rhythms you will be more productive. *NOTE: using your natural rhythms doesn't mean ignoring the vital information about sleep that we discussed earlier – you still need your sleep and if you think your peak time is 3am you may need to change your*

*rhythm to allow time for sleep. Yes, you can*
*change your natural rhythms.*

### Establishing a Routine

To establish a routine, you need to have a weekly timetable. We'll talk about those in more detail later but for now you just need to know that creating a 'timetable' of your personal time (just like they do at school) will enable you to have things that you do on a regular basis, such as each night. Putting this down on a timetable will keep you accountable and enable you to get these activities/tasks completed without too much thought and energy.

Firstly, think about the things that you do regularly. Are you a part of a sport which requires regular practise or a club which has regular meetings? Do you exercise often? (Your answer to that should be YES!) Do you have regular family, religious/spiritual or personal time? What about chores? Get the idea? When you list all the things you need to do you can place them on a timetable and make them a part of a routine.

Next, once you have your activities/tasks listed you can decide when to do what and prioritise your list. Rather than starting with your most important task first (as you would with goals) think about which task compliments other tasks. For example, rather than blocking two study periods together separate them with some chores to act as a study break. Continue this until your routine is fixed and ready to try. Now you can begin turning your routines into habits. Remember that routines are not set in concrete – they can be changed, so if it doesn't suit you modify it and try again – just don't give up!

## Ask Questions

There is an old saying – "there's no such thing as a stupid question" and it is doubly true for those wanting to succeed at high school. For most students asking a question in class is not popular. The reasons for this may include: it's not 'cool'; if you ask a question you must be 'dumb'; questions make the class last longer; those who ask questions are 'sucking up' to the teacher; or it's just uncomfortable. These are reasons that may seem important but have little real value. Think about what we have discussed so far – are you going to sacrifice your success because other students will laugh at you, or think you're not cool? Are you going to remain ignorant because asking a question may feel uncomfortable? You cannot let such unhelpful thoughts and feelings get in the way of your success!

Despite what many students may think, asking questions is the smart thing to do – it is the only way for an ignorant person to cease being ignorant. For you to overcome your natural ignorance (*note: there is nothing bad about being ignorant – ignorance is just not knowing something. The problem arises when someone chooses to remain ignorant*). To be successful you must develop the habit of asking questions. If there is an equation that you do not understand, a sentence that you cannot follow, a process that you do not remember, or anything that you do not know that you feel you must know you must ask a question. Let's look at the best way to do that.

Firstly, you must know whom to ask. In school the most obvious person to ask is your teacher. Your teacher knows you, knows what you are supposed to be learning and how best to provide you with that information. In most cases your teacher will want to help you because, let's face it – the more successful you are the better they look. Just take the following ideas into account:

- Ask your question outside of class. Unless your question is directly related to the discussion at hand asking a question during class can be distracting for a teacher, and many will not have the time to answer questions in class. So, approach the teacher after class or during a break then they will be able to focus their attention on your question.

- Write down your question before asking it. By writing your question down you will clarify it to yourself and ensure that you express it clearly to your teacher.

- Write down the answer and repeat it to your teacher. When you have received your answer, write it down, read it and make sure you understand it. When you are sure that you understand the answer repeat it to your teacher and ask for clarification. That way there will be no confusion and less misunderstanding.

- Do not quit until you have an answer. Some students make the mistake of asking the question only once – even if they do not yet understand the answer. If you do not understand the answer that the teacher has given you ask again – tell them you do not understand. Do not nod, smile and say you understand when you don't. This will give the teacher the impression that you understand and make it harder to find the answer later. So, tell them that you do not understand, that you need clarification, that you need further explanation.

Tell them whatever you need to until you find the answer to your question.

If you have not received an answer from your teacher, or you are unable to ask your teacher, who else can you go to? You can try another teacher, you can try another adult (parent, librarian, other family member, etc.), you can ask your friends or you can search on the Internet. Just remember that if you ask your friends or the Internet you must verify the accuracy of the answers you receive – your friends may be great but they do not know everything, and never trust the Internet without checking multiple sources (we'll talk more about this later).

If you are able to make asking questions a habit you will find that a number of things have changed: Firstly, you will begin to know more – you will gain a reputation as someone who is smart and intelligent (unlike those who think that only stupid people ask questions!); Secondly, your teachers will start to recognise in you someone who cares about their work and wants to do better – they will appreciate your effort and enthusiasm; thirdly, your standard of work will improve – once you have clarified the things you are unsure of your work will begin to be just what the teachers are looking for; and lastly, you will become more confident in yourself and your own work.

## Reading

One of the most important habits you can develop to help you be successful at high school is reading. The average person reads less than one book a year but successful people read dozens of books each year – this is doubly true for students. If you want to be successful then you must make reading a habit. For some of you this will not be a problem but for many of you making reading a habit will be difficult, but that should not stop you from developing it anyway.

So, what are the benefits of reading?

- Reading provides mental stimulation – just like the muscles in your body your brain needs exercise, and it is only exercised by use. Reading is one of the best ways to stimulate your brain, making it more agile and better able to process. Just like with physical workouts, the more you read the stronger your brain will become.
- Reading improves concentration – by being stimulated your brain increases its ability to concentrate. Not only does reading increase and strengthen the neurons in your brain but the process of sitting still and focusing on the words

161

on the page increases your ability to concentrate for longer periods of time – a necessity if you are planning to be successful in high school.

- Reading improves memory – the process of reading strengthens the neural pathways in your brain and makes thinking easier and more effective. One of the results of this is improved memory. Being able to recall information is a process that can be learned, developed and improved and reading is one of the activities that can help you achieve this – especially if you are reading about improving your memory!

- Reading expands vocabulary – one of the characteristics of successful people is a larger vocabulary than the average person – basically, they know more words and how to use them. One of the very best ways to increase your vocabulary is by reading. As a teacher of English for more than 20 years I have always been able to identify those students who read more than the other students – they always had a more advanced vocabulary than their peers. They knew words that other students in the same class didn't and they were able to use those words correctly. This was a direct result of reading.

- Reading improves language – another characteristic of successful people is excellent communication and language skills. Reading also helps improve this. When you read you are being exposed to different forms of language (especially if you read a variety of books) and the more exposure you have the more you 'absorb' that language. Your own language skills develop as a result, and your ability to communicate improves. This is also vital for students who are not native English speakers – read lots of English books and your English skills will improve.

- Reading increases knowledge – in addition to an improved vocabulary, students who read more, know more. There is a clear correlation between reading and increased knowledge. The reason for this is that reading expands the reader's scope of experience – you see, hear and do more, you visit more places, and you meet and interact with more people – even if it is all vicariously! This translates into more knowledge and experience, much of which can be directly related to life – depending on what you read.

- Reading improves writing – it makes sense that reading is linked to writing, after all, to read you focus on someone else's writing. It also means that if you read a variety of books, by a variety of authors, on a variety of topics you will be exposed to a variety of writing styles. You will see writing that works well and writing that doesn't. You will see how words can be used to evoke emotion and create effective visual images. You will see how words can be used to persuade, argue, describe, explain and entertain. All this exposure will translate into your own improved writing.

- Reading reduces stress – the physical act of sitting still and focusing on a page reduces your heart rate and calms you down. In addition, by focusing on what the words are saying you will lose focus on whatever is causing you stress. This may not work if reading has not become a habit for you – in fact, you may find it difficult to concentrate on the page if you are stressed about something. If that's the case, get up, go for a walk and try again later. When reading becomes a habit you will find that sitting down with a good book will wash away all other thoughts for the present.

- Reading helps you sleep better – because reading helps you to relax it is an ideal promoter of sleep. I have lost count of the times that I have been unable to sleep, picked up a book I was currently reading and within minutes could not keep my eyes open. Reading slows your body down and makes the transition to sleep easier and quicker. Make reading a part of your sleep process and you will find that not only are you reading more but you are sleeping better. Try it!

- Reading is what successful people do – copying successful people is a sure way to become successful like them. Think about it, if you do what your favourite sportsman does you will improve in that sport, if you do what your favourite artist does you will improve in that area. Emulate successful people and you become like them. This is reason enough (despite all the great reasons above) to read more – because successful people do it! Copy them and you will become like them.

Now that you know the benefits of reading you need to think about what to read. To be successful you need to ensure that you are reading the right things. Comics and anime may be enjoyable for some people but are not really going to advance your education too far. The same goes for blogs, newspapers, most magazines and websites. They may be interesting and have some educational value but they are not the type of writing you want to focus on. Fiction books (including, science-fiction, fantasy, romance, horror, suspense and other novels) are a great way to relax and escape. These should be a part of your reading habit but it is a good idea to read a variety of novels, that is, don't read only fantasy novels – read a fantasy novel, then a romance novel, then a suspense novel, etc. This will give you a variety of 'experiences' and expose you to a variety of writing styles.

The best category of books to read is non-fiction. These are books about real-life things and are limitless. Reading about subjects that you are studying at school is the best way to be successful. For example, if you are taking History at school find history books about the era you are studying (such as World War Two, or Classical Rome). Reading these books will give you a context that will catapult you to the front of the class in understanding. If you are reading one book each term for each of the subjects you study at school your understanding and knowledge will set you far above your peers – and maybe even your teachers.

It is also a great idea to read biographies – books about famous people. Learning about other people (it can be people who are still alive (like Queen Elizabeth II) or long dead (like George Washington)) is an excellent way to learn from the mistakes of others. The more we learn from others the more wisdom and knowledge we gain. You will find that you are developing positive habits and taking helpful advice from people you have never met, and you will be better for it! So, read as much as you can, in great variety and you, and those around you, will notice the difference.

- *ACTION — sign-up to Goodreads at www.goodreads.com This is where you can keep track of the books you have read and those that you want to read. You can also interact with other readers from across the world. NOTE: never share your personal information with anyone on these social networks.*

## Habits Action Plan

1. Determine to begin regular progress reviews today. Mark in your calendar the times for yearly and termly reviews and add time for the weekly and daily reviews to your timetable.
2. Purchase a planner (if you don't already have one) and begin using it as a primary organisational tool.
3. Purchase a wall calendar (if you don't already have one) and begin using it as a primary organisational tool.

4. Begin the process of eliminating or reducing distractions in your life. Don't wait, get started now!

# Part 5 – Environment

## *The environment shapes people's actions*

*B.F. Skinner*

We've spent a lot of time focusing on you – inside and outside – and that is because you are the most important factor when it comes to your own success in high school. You are the most important, but not the only factor – another factor which is important is your environment. Where you are, can have a great impact on what you are doing and how well you are doing it. We will spend this part of the book looking at how you can maximise your environment to help you be successful.

Why is environment so important? Think about it – you may have the best attitude, a positive lifestyle, awesome goals and excellent habits but if you are trying to study in the middle of a busy city train station you will not be too successful. An exaggeration, I know, but the principle is the same – you want to create an environment that will give you the best opportunity to be effective and efficient – to make your success as easy as possible. Let's look at some ideas that can help you achieve that.

# A Place for Study

It is important that you have a dedicated place where you do your study and work. Lots of students do their work where ever they happen to be at the time – sometimes in the lounge room, sometimes in the kitchen, outside in the garden if it's a nice day. The problem with this is that it's more difficult to develop the correct frame of mind for study, there may be too many distractions and equipment that you need may not be available (also, review what we said earlier about cognitive load).

Your 'frame of mind' is vital to effective study. Your frame of mind refers to what you are ready to do. Obviously when you want to study you need to be in the frame of mind for focus and concentration. This doesn't happen automatically and it isn't the case all the time – it must be cultivated and encouraged. Let's look at an example: it's Saturday night, you've just returned home from a party where there was a lot of friends, loud music, good food and laughter. You are pumped and full of energy. Do you feel ready to sit down and read a good book? I don't think so, because you're not in the right frame of mind.

That's why having one place in the house that is "your study place" is a good idea. Having a place where you always do your work puts you in the right frame of mind. Every time you sit down to start your work your subconscious mind readies your brain for thinking, focus and concentration. Just like if you walk into your bedroom your brain should begin to prepare for sleep.

Having a regular place to study is also important to ensure that the 'tools of your trade' are available and close. Just like a builder wants to keep his hammer within reach and a fisherman wants to be within reach of his rod, a student (that is your occupation) needs to have their tools close – this includes paper, pens, pencils, erasers, highlighters, books, computer (for research, not gaming or messaging!!!), etc. What you want to avoid is a trek through the house to find a replacement pen when you are in the middle of an important paragraph or idea.

## Distractions

Another important requirement of your work environment is a lack of distractions. It may seem obvious but many (if not most) students attempt to complete work and study where there are too many distractions. Whether it's the TV, family members, a messaging app, music or a range of other sights and sounds, distractions are going to seriously hamper your chances of success in high school. Does that mean that you won't succeed if you listen to music while you work? No. Does it mean that you will fail if your apartment happens to be next to an all-night supermarket with a bright yellow flashing neon sign? Not at all. But it does mean that with these distractions you will not be as successful as you could have been if you had studied in a peaceful, distraction-free environment.

To best prepare yourself for success in high school you need to eliminate or reduce anything which can distract you from your task at hand – your work and study. That will mean a careful audit of the place you plan to make your study space. You will need to look around and ask yourself what will distract you from focusing on your work. Obviously electronic devices need to be turned off or put out of sight and hearing, if there are posters on the walls that are distracting, you may need to move or cover them. If there is something distracting out the window you may need to close or cover it. If there are distracting noises you may need to close the door or block them out in other ways. Everything needs to be analysed until you can be sure that when you are working you will be able to focus solely on your tasks.

Sometimes it's not possible to eliminate some distractions. This could be because they are out of your control (noisy neighbours) or it's too difficult (you share a room with a sibling). Either way there are still things that you can do to reduce the impact of distractions on you. You can try moving to another room, using a pair of noise-cancelling headphones, or changing the time that you study. If these don't work you may need to be more creative. Whatever you do, don't let the distractions get the better of you – your success is too important for that.

## Comfort

When you choose a place to study you need to take comfort into account. This is obvious but sometimes for the wrong reasons. Many students study in the most comfortable place they can find – their bed – but this is not a good idea. Being too comfortable can be counter-productive and reduce how effective you are. You should choose a place which is a nice balance between comfort and practicality. A work desk and chair is ideal – avoid couches or sofas, beanbags, hammocks or other items of furniture that were designed for relaxation. You want your study place to get you into the 'frame of mind' for work, not sleep.

Consider the temperature of your study place. Once again you must aim for a balance. If it is too warm you will feel lethargic and struggle to stay awake, but if it is too cold you will not be able to concentrate on your work. A room temperature of around 20° C (68 ° F) is ideal for getting work done. If you need to add or subtract an extra layer of clothing, do so, but resist the temptation to pump up the heater or cooler. If you have no control over the temperature then you will have to wear clothing that is appropriate to keep you comfortable but alert.

When you are choosing a chair for your study place find one that is comfortable for your size – avoid a chair that is too high or too short. An incorrectly sized chair will cause you to adopt a bad posture – this will not only reduce your effectiveness but may also have long-term physical consequences. Find a chair that is height-adjustable. If you can, get a chair with wheels – that will enable you to be mobile and flexible. Find one that is well-cushioned because you will be spending many hours on it.

## Light

Another factor to consider when choosing your place to study is light. Obviously, you won't get much done in a dark room, but too many students try to study in a room which is too dark. Conversely, a room which is too bright is better, but still not ideal. The most effective lighting for a study room is bright but not too bright – in practical terms that would be a little less than what you would find on a typical summer's day. A bright room will enable you to see your work clearly and will be easier on your eyes — they won't have to strain or squint because of too much or not enough light.

A bright room will also make you feel better. Darkness is closely associated with depression for good reason. When you are feeling 'dark' you are not as productive as when you are feeling 'bright'. Remember when we talked about attitude earlier? Being in a bright room will not only help you feel better but will also promote more positive feelings in an upward spiral. You will feel better and do better work because of it.

The best way to control the light in your study place is with globes or lamps. If you are able, find a bright one that is as close to natural daylight as possible. These days LED lights are more expensive but last much longer and, if possible, fluorescent globes should be avoided.

## Noise

An effective environment is a quiet one. Despite what you may have heard, or what you think, you work best when you can concentrate without noise distractions — that includes music. I've heard many students say that they work better with music playing, or the TV on in the background, but science says that's not the case. Studies have shown that in some cases music is okay, but in most others it makes working effectively harder. Try, as much as possible to work in silence, especially when you are trying to concentrate, or if you can't, at least try to minimise any noise.

## Environment Action Plan

1. Find a place that you can adopt as 'your study place'. It may be in your house or the local library. Either way, make sure you consistently use this each time you study.

2. Choose a chair that will be your 'study chair'. This will be the only chair that you study in and is kept in 'your study place'. If you can purchase a new chair, try them in a study posture before you buy.

# Part 6 – Planning and Organisation

*Failing to plan is planning to fail.*

*Alan Lakein*

Now we get to what is probably one of the most important parts of this book – what you do <u>before</u> the work starts! This may sound a bit strange to you but I have found over the years that those people (and students) who plan, generally succeed. Planning is probably the most important element of work and study and if you don't do it you will wander around, lost and not aware of what you are doing.

It is commonly believed that any planning or preparation that takes place before a task begins will enable the task to be completed quicker and easier – regardless of whether you are writing a story or essay, preparing an assignment or presentation, or studying for an exam. By starting straight into the task without planning (or by doing minimal planning) you are setting yourself up to fail, or at least receive a lower result than if you had planned.

Let's look at some of the important factors of planning and organisation – the practises that will enable you to work smarter, not harder.

# Before the Year Starts

There are many things you could do before your school years starts. While the other students are enjoying the last few weeks of the holidays you could be preparing to succeed. This may not seem like a great way to start your year but remember that two weeks into the school year your friends' holidays will be forgotten but your preparation will already be giving you many advantages.

**Contact your Teachers**

Firstly, try to contact your new teachers. Sometimes you will be aware of who will be teaching you in the new year – you may even already know them – but often you will not. Make it a priority to find out who they are and talk to them if you can. Most schools begin the school-year earlier for teachers than they do for students (yes, teachers have less holidays than you) and a quick call to the school will often get you the information you need. Ask if you can visit the school before classes start to talk with your teachers (or if you can't – talk with them over the phone).

What do you talk about?

- Introduce yourself – tell them briefly who you are;
- Inform them that you are determined to succeed;
- Ask them what you need to do to prepare for their class;
- Ask them if there is any extra reading you can do before classes start;
- Thank them for their time;

You will find that teachers will generally be pleased to find one of their students being so proactive and taking it upon themselves to make this call. This will not only get you the information that you need but will, more importantly, give them a positive impression of you before the year even starts. That way they will be more likely to assist you in your desire for success throughout the year.

- *ACTION – make a list of all your teachers for the next year. Don't know who they will be? Call the school and ask for the information. Review your list and prioritise it – for example, there may be teachers that you already know so you can see them first, some teachers may be out of town until school starts again. Once your list is prioritised start at the top and see each teacher as soon as you can.*

## Get Booklists

One of the things that you need to get from your new teachers is booklists – this is (as the name suggests) a list of books that will be used during the year. Some schools provide all the books that a student needs, while others provide a booklist and students must buy the books themselves. Whichever methods your school uses try to get a list of the books you will be using so that you can familiarise yourself with all the books before classes start.

## Read Texts

Once you have a list of the books you will be using during the school year you should begin to read them as early as you can. There are basically two types of books that are used in schools: textbooks and literary texts, and these must be read in different ways. A typical textbook is a Science or Mathematics textbook. A typical literary text is a novel, play or short story.

A textbook is not something that should be read through like a novel. Instead, read through the table of contents to familiarise yourself with the topics that will be covered during the year. Are there any that you are already aware of? Are any of them completely unknown to you? Examine each topic separately by reading the introduction to the chapter and scanning through the pages to briefly view the explanations, examples, pictures and exercises. This should take only a few minutes but it will give you an overview of the content. You will also find that once you have seen the information your subconscious mind will begin to process it and when you cover it in class you will find it easier to understand.

*NOTE: if your school has digital textbooks you may be able to get a copy earlier or a second-hand paper version. If not, concentrate on your other subjects for now and review your digital books when you receive them.*

A literary text is a book that is studied for its literary qualities and content rather than just a means of passing on information. *Great Expectations* by Charles Dickens, and *Romeo and Juliet* by William Shakespeare are two well-known examples. We will look at the best reading strategies later but basically you should aim to have all your literary texts read through before classes start for the year. READ ALL OF THEM?!! I hear your scream! If you are serious about being successful then yes, all of them.

To achieve this, you must do two things: start early and read every day. If you can start reading your literary texts well before the school year starts you will be well on the way to completing them – even if you don't manage to read all of them. You don't have to read them all at the same time – start with one (preferably the one you will be studying first in class) and focus on it until it's finished, then start the next one. If you spend 30 minutes reading each morning, and 30 minutes each evening it will take you about a week to read most novels studied in school. 30 minutes is not much time and if you are still on holidays you should be able to find the extra time.

*Remember: if you've made a commitment to succeed at high school the work doesn't start on the first day of school – nor does it finish on the last day of school. If that's what you expect then you should probably stop reading this book right now. Because you've read this far I think you are committed, so focus on the new successful you and start reading!*

- *ACTION – make a reading list of all the books you must read for the year. Prioritise the list according to when books are to be studied. Now you know the time frames you have for your reading.*

### Organise a Calendar

The next thing that you need to do before classes start is organise your calendar. Your calendar should have the following:

- The term dates of your school year.
- When the year starts and finishes and all term breaks.
- Any public holidays.
- All your personal events (birthdays, etc.).

Once all this information has been added to your calendar you are ready for the year to begin. Your calendar will be one of your best friends during the year so ensure that you tell it everything – that is, add all school and personal events to it. We'll talk more about your calendar soon.

## Time Management

One of the best ways to succeed is to learn how to manage your time. Time management is a characteristic of all successful people. It refers to being able to use your time wisely and not waste it. The fact that most people waste up to eight hours each day shows the importance of time management. So, what exactly is wasted time? Any time that you are doing something that doesn't directly relate to your success is probably a waste of your time. Does that mean you can't relax or have fun? Not at all. But it does mean that you plan the use of your time so that relaxation and fun are balanced with working towards your goals. Remember, to be successful everything must be on purpose, not accidental.

## Time Audit

Before you can learn to manage your time more effectively you must be aware of how you currently use your time. To learn this, you need to conduct a 'time audit' – an analysis of how you use the minutes of a typical day. Just like an accountant audits the finances of a business, you must audit your own time-use.

To do this you must create an audit sheet. This is simply a piece of paper on which you draw a table with three columns: one for the time, another for how you use that time and a third to analyse your time use. See the example below:

| 6:30 am | Wake, drink water and stretch | yes |
|---------|-------------------------------|-----|
| 6:40 am | Have breakfast | yes |
| 6:50 am | Watch some morning cartoons | no |
| 7:00 am | Have a shower and get dressed | yes |
| 7:10 am | Prepare for day | yes |

As you can see the example has the day divided into 10 minute blocks. Start at the time you wake up and continue through to when you go to sleep. It may be easier to create this in MS WORD or EXCEL then print out enough for a week.

Once you have a week's worth of audit sheets begin to record each activity that you do in that 10-minute period. First block out all those activities that you do on a regular basis that you have no control over, like school, travelling on the bus, sports training, etc. For everything else you should record your activity for that 10-minute block of time. It doesn't matter if you are not totally accurate – if you can get an idea of your average time usage, but you must be totally honest. Don't record that you were doing homework when you were watching TV – this is not being done to impress anyone but to get an accurate picture of your time usage.

Once you have completed recording your time usage for the day go through your list and assess whether the entry is positive (helps you to reach your goals) or negative (doesn't help you reach your goals). In the above example having breakfast helps you reach your goals by ensuring that you are fed and have enough energy for the day, but watching cartoons doesn't help you reach your goals.

After completing your time audit for the week look at it to determine how effectively you use your time. Ask yourself the following questions:

- As a proportion of my day – how much time do I waste?
- Are some days better than others? If so, why are they different?
- How much time do I waste each day?
- How much more would I be able to achieve if I didn't waste as much time as I do?

The next step after a time audit is to determine how you are going to use your time differently (here I am assuming that your time audit showed that you waste a lot of your time because most people do).

## Goals

To use your time more wisely you must know what your goals are. We discussed goals earlier, so you should know what's involved, and be able to create long term and short term, effective goals. Only with these goals in front of you it is possible to plan your time more effectively, because if you don't know where you are going you will not know how to get there.

Once you know what your main goals are you should divide them into groups that coincide with the main areas of your life, such as health goals, school goals, relationship goals, etc. Ideally, there should be a good spread of goals – you don't want to be putting your energy into achieving goals in only one area of your life, that will lead to an unbalanced life and problems in the future.

Now that you can identify the main goals that you are working towards take another look at the results of your time audit and analyse how much of your time is spent on achieving your goals. For example, if losing weight is one of your health goals and going for a 30-minute walk is one of the activities on your time audit then you know that you have spent some time working towards achieving that goal on that day. It is best if you can spend some time every day working on each of your major goals that will maintain some consistency and build positive habits. You should aim to spend most of your time working towards any one of your goals. If you are not doing that you are wasting your time.

### Task Prioritising
The best way to improve your time management is to prioritise your time. This means you must put your activities into order of importance and ensuring that you are spending the right time on the right tasks. Look at your goals and prioritise them in order of importance.

Think about which one you would like to instantly achieve tomorrow if a genie gave you one wish – that is probably your most important goal. Keep going like this until you have all your goals in order of importance.

Ideally, it would be best if you could spend the most time on your most important goal, but that is not always possible. Some goals are long term and require a balanced, long-term approach to achieve. Other goals are time-based and require a concentrated effort for a specific period. Take all of this into account when you consider how best to use your time.

The next step is to put all you have learned in this process onto a calendar and into a planner.

## Personal Calendar

Assuming you have read the section on organising your calendar you will have a calendar with all your personal and general information on it ready to go before classes start. Now you need to consider the analysis that you have just completed of your goals and think about how you can integrate that into your weeks and months. You have several options.

If you have a goal that involves achieving something by a particular date, mark that date on your calendar (if it isn't marked already). You can spread out your preparation from now until that date to ensure that you are working towards the goal consistently and not leaving it until the last minute.

If you have a goal that involves a consistent condition (such a maintaining a certain level of fitness) that you want as a part of your life, you can mark regular sessions on your calendar to work towards that goal. This way you can be consistent and make it a habit. That will ensure that it becomes a part of your life.

A basic principle of time management is that you spend more time on the things that are important to you. This is often an unconscious decision, but you must make it a conscious one. For example, if you say that your health is a high priority to you but you only spend a few minutes a week exercising, then it is clearly not that important; and if you say that success in school is important but you spend most of your free time watching TV then you are lying to yourself. Once you know what is important to you determine to spend much of your time focusing on that area.

Obviously, the focus of this book is success in high school so the expectation is that you will be devoting a large portion of your time to that goal. Your calendar should reflect that by having some time each day set aside for building your success in high school. The next step is focusing your attention from the year or term calendar to a weekly timetable.

## Personal Timetable

A calendar helps you to see the 'big picture' of the year or term but it is no good for focusing your vision on the present – for that you need a timetable. A personal timetable is your organisation for the week, helping you to break up your term into more manageable pieces.

*NOTE: An effective timetable is practical and personal – you cannot use one that someone else has designed (not without modifying it to suit yourself) and yours is of limited value to others. That's why I have included an example timetable for you to see how they work and a blank one for you to make your own.*

First, let's talk about the value of timetables. Timetables are used throughout society to organise time: trains, planes and buses use timetables, government and the military use timetables, and, of course, schools and universities use them. The common idea is that a timetable ensures that time is used more effectively when there are clear and planned schedules. Imagine what it would be like at school if there were no timetables. It would be fun and relaxing for a while but eventually you would realise that your time is being wasted and nothing is being learned.

Your personal timetable is the same – without it you will still get things done, but you would waste a lot of time and not get your important tasks completed, or they wouldn't be as good as if you used a timetable.

Let's look at an example of a personal timetable:

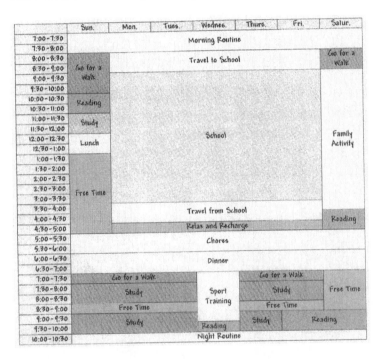

Notice the following things:

- Try to start each morning at about the same time (yes, even the weekends);
- Use colours to make your timetable easier to read and remember;
- If you want your timetable to be more precise you can use 15 minute blocks rather than the 30 minute blocks in this example;
- Notice that some activities are repeated each day at the same time and can be combined across the week;
- Some activities (like dinner, family time and chores) will have to be negotiated with your family;

*Remember: this is just an example – yours may be very different, depending upon your own priorities and circumstances.*

*NOTE: It is important to keep to the times that you have set in your calendar. If you don't, you will find that you naturally revert to doing things that are fun but not productive.*

One of the first things to do when you are constructing a personal timetable is to block out the non-negotiable times (such as school, travel time and dinner time, etc.), these are the activities over which you have no control.

Once that is done you can fit in the other activities based on priority – family time, study, exercise, etc.

Once you have developed your personal timetable put it up where you can easily see it and share it with your family. Then the challenge will be to try it out for a few weeks. You may need to modify it until it suits perfectly but ensure that you do not give up. It will take a few weeks to really make an impact so persist and you will see the benefits.

## Study Timetable

Once you have a personal timetable you have a clear picture of what your week looks like but you will need a more detailed timetable to organise your study. This can be achieved with a study timetable. A study timetable helps you manage your study more effectively. It can be integrated into a personal timetable, or it can be separate – it's up to you.

A study timetable is simply a timetable organising the time in the afternoons and evenings (and weekends, too) when you do your study. It is usually set between the hours of 4-10pm, but that is flexible. If you have a personal timetable your study timetable fits right into it. Let's look at an example:

| | Sun. | Mon. | Tues. | Wednes. | Thurs. | Fri. | Satur. |
|---|---|---|---|---|---|---|---|
| 7:00-7:30 | Go for a Walk | | | Sport Training | Go for a Walk | | Free Time |
| 7:30-8:00 | English | English | English | | English | English | |
| 8:00-8:30 | Science | Science | Science | | Science | Science | |
| 8:30-9:00 | Free Time | | | | Free Time | | |
| 9:00-9:30 | Maths | Maths | Maths | | Maths | | Reading |
| 9:30-10:00 | History | Geography | Health | Reading | Technology | | |

Notice the following things:

- Colour-coding your study sessions makes then easier to remember and follow;
- Study sessions are made up of 30 minute blocks because that is a good period to stay focused without becoming tired. Any longer and you may lose focus, any shorter and you may not get much done;
- Rather than doing a large study block of one subject (for example, English) they have been spread across the week. This adds variety to your study sessions and enables you to better remember what you are working on because you are working on it daily, not every few days, or once a week;
- Try to keep one day each week study-free. Remember the rest day we talked about earlier;
- Treat reading as another subject – that's how important it is! However, that doesn't mean you only have to read school-related books during these times.

The real value of a study timetable is that you force yourself to be disciplined when it comes to getting your study done and you spread your work out over the week. No more spending five hours starting and finishing an assignment the night before it is due! Now you can spread those hours over weeks and do a much better job.

We'll look at exactly how to use your study time later. Now, let's look at how you break up your projects into more manageable pieces.

## Breaking up Projects

One of the best ways to organise your time is to not work on large projects – sounds too good to be true? Don't get too excited because I don't mean that you shouldn't work on projects that are large, but rather that any large projects you work on should be reduced to smaller projects. We briefly mentioned this when we talked about procrastination. Let me explain.

You have a major assignment due for History in which you must explore the causes of the First World War and it's supposed to be 2,000 words in length. Sounds overwhelming, doesn't it! Think about it – 2,000 words is about seven pages. How can you possibly write an essay that's seven pages long? Impossible! Don't worry, when you nail all the processes and habits that we talk about in this book a 2,000-word essay will not be a problem.

When you look at a large task in this way it is easy to get discouraged, overwhelmed and fail before you even start. The trick is to change your perspective – don't look at the big problem, look at the pieces that make up the big problem – they are much smaller.

Think about this: one of the causes of the First World War was the naval arms race. It's relatively easy to research what that was – a race between Great Britain and Germany to produce more large battleships – and then write 200-300 words describing it, explaining it, and giving examples. That's one cause done and you are already 10-15% of the way through your essay.

Cause number two was the alliance system – the two sides created alliances with other empires meaning that if one was drawn into the war they all would be. Again, it would be easy enough to write 200-300 words describing, explaining, and giving examples for this cause. Now you are more than 20% through your essay. Do the same for 6 or 7 more causes add an introduction and conclusion and the first draft of your 'impossible' essay would be completed.

We will be looking at essay writing in more detail later, but this serves as an example of how a large task can be made more manageable when it is reduced to smaller parts – rather than writing a 2,000 word essay you have written six 300 words essays and put them together. This can be done with any type of project. A portfolio needs to be created – break it down into its component parts and do each one separately. A presentation needs to be prepared – prepare and practise each part separately before you put them together. Any large task can be made easier by breaking it up into smaller parts. Just remember that once this has been done you will have to put it all back together to make sure it is consistent and fits well.

## Planning and Organisation Action Plan

1. Ensure that you have a calendar with all your important dates, events and tasks included.
2. Conduct a time audit on how you used your time today. Was today productive or not?
3. Create a personal timetable to organise your time each day.
4. Create a study timetable to organise your study time each night.

# Part 7 – Homework

*My parents always taught me that my day job would never make me rich; it'd be my homework.*

*Daymond John*

Homework! It's a word that ruins every student's afternoon and smashes their dreams of a relaxing night on the couch. But homework doesn't have to be a bad word – in fact if you are interested in success at high school you will need to become very familiar with homework. The basic fact is that there is not enough spare time at school for you to get all the required work completed. This may seem obvious, but many students (and people in general – including teachers) have an incorrect understanding of homework.

Arguments have been raging for years in educational circles about whether homework is 'good' or 'bad', 'useful' or 'harmful' and whether it should be stopped or encouraged. But the simple fact is that homework is necessary if you want to succeed at high school. It should not be looked on as something extra but as an extension of school – an opportunity to build on and explore more deeply what was learned during the day. That sounds like a privilege, not a burden, to me.

In this section, we will look at how homework can help you be more effective, and how it can ultimately reduce the time you spend on work at home.

## Types of Homework

Firstly, it is important to recognise that homework is not simply 'work you do at home'. Yes, it is that, but it is also more than that. Homework is your opportunity to do the following:

- internalise what you learned at school;
- personalise how you use what you learned at school;
- complete and reinforce what you learned at school;
- commit what you learned at school to memory;
- do your best in school-related tasks;
- plan future tasks;
- prepare for future success;

It sounds like a lot of positive outcomes from a little bit of homework, so let's look at the details.

### Work Not Completed in Class

The first role of homework is to give you the opportunity to complete work that wasn't finished at school. This is probably also the most important part – having those gaps in your learning is 'bad!" There may be many different reasons why work was not completed at school:

- you ran out of time;
- you weren't in the class (excursion, illness, etc.);
- the teacher didn't give the work until the end of the class;
- there was a school event that interrupted the class;
- you needed resources that weren't available in the class to complete the task;
- there were too many distractions in the class;
- you were messing around in the class – this one obviously doesn't apply to you but I added it to reinforce that you should always be focused and on-task in class!

Suffice it to say that there will be times that you will have incomplete work from school that needs to be completed. You should ensure that the work is always completed – even if the teacher is not going to check it – after all, are you doing this for the teacher or for yourself?

So, your first task should be to ensure that you are aware of what needs to be completed (that should be written in your planner) and that it becomes a priority to complete it. This work should not take up a lot of your time and can be done in the first part of your study session for each subject (more on that later).

## Revision of Class Work

Once the unfinished class work has been completed some time must be spent on revising what was learned in class. Revision is vital to embed facts, ideas and principles into your long-term memory.

Let's take a moment to talk about your memory: you have two types of memory – short term and long term. Your short-term memory lasts only about a day – it is used to help you filter your memories whilst you sleep. Under normal circumstances your short-term memory is wiped clean every day. Your long-term memory (what enables you to remember what happened during that day at the beach last year) is a little bit more selective than your short-term memory. Basically, those thoughts that you dwell on, and think about repeatedly will be kept in your long-term memory. This means that you will remember them a long time afterwards. To purposefully embed something into your long-term memory (like facts for an exam) it is important to review it multiple times in the days after it is first learned. Therefore, revising your class work is important.

When you come home after a day of school you have a head filled with all the information you learned during your classes. If you do nothing, that information will gradually fade away after a day or two – it will be replaced by all the new information that you learn the following day.

You must purposefully review that information to ensure that you remember it. This is done in a variety of ways:

- reread the notes you took during class – this will place the information at the forefront of your mind;
- Rewrite the notes you took during class – this will reinforce and clarify the information in your mind;
- Summarise the notes to highlight the main ideas – this will force you to focus on the important information;
- Read through your summary notes the following day – this will begin to embed the information into your long-term memory;
- Read through the summary notes a week later to guarantee the information will embed into your long-term memory;

These steps may seem like a complicated way to remember things but they are simple and easy to do, especially if they are a part of your study program.

Depending on how many notes you took in class this process should not take you too long but you will be grateful that you followed it when you need to recall the information later.

### Work on Assignments

Now we get to the time when you work on the assignments that were given in class that are due later. These tasks sometimes require the most self-discipline because their due dates are so far in the future. It is easier to ignore them until just before they are due, but that would be a mistake. To be successful in any task you must plan and complete it in advance – that will give you plenty of opportunity to check your work for errors or make improvements before it is submitted.

Previously we discussed the benefits of breaking up your large projects into smaller, more manageable ones. This is where that process really pays off! Now that you have broken your project into smaller pieces and spread those pieces out over a period of weeks or months (but still well within the deadline) you can focus on completing each individual piece rather than worrying about the whole. It also means that you don't need a large block of time to complete the whole task in one sitting because you only have the smaller one to complete.

Let's look at a practical example of how this is done: You must complete a project on a famous scientist and you've chosen Albert Einstein. You can divide your project up into the following sections: Introduction, childhood and early years, his beliefs and ideas, early research, later research, and his legacy. For each section, you will have to do the following things: reading and research, take notes, organise the notes, find images, write your first draft. After these sections have been completed and your first draft is written you will need to edit it, finalise presentation and check your work, hopefully multiple times. A rough plan of the entire process might look like this:

1. Reading and research for introduction
2. Take notes for introduction
3. Organise the introduction notes
4. Find images for introduction
5. Write first draft of introduction
6. Reading and research for childhood and early years
7. Take notes for childhood and early years
8. Organise the childhood and early years notes

9.  Find images for childhood and early years
10. Write first draft of childhood and early years
11. Reading and research for his beliefs and ideas
12. Take notes for his beliefs and ideas
13. Organise his beliefs and ideas notes
14. Find images for his beliefs and ideas
15. Write first draft of his beliefs and ideas
16. Reading and research for early research
17. Take notes for early research
18. Organise the early research notes
19. Find images for early research
20. Write first draft of early research
21. Reading and research for later research
22. Take notes for later research
23. Organise the later research notes
24. Find images for later research
25. Write first draft of later research
26. Reading and research for his legacy
27. Take notes for his legacy
28. Organise his legacy notes
29. Find images for his legacy
30. Write first draft of his legacy
31. Edit first draft
32. Finalise presentation
33. First check of project
34. Second check of project (done by parents)

35.   Final check of project

Say that you were given the project in the second week of this term and it is due at the end of next term – that gives you about 20 weeks including term breaks. If you plan to complete two sessions of this project each week (that's about 1 hour each week) you will complete the project with about two weeks to spare. Not only will your project be finished early but it will be well-planned, well-organised and it will look great. And, importantly, you haven't dropped everything else to focus on this one project – you still have plenty of time each week to work on other things.

Remember, this is just an example, and how you organise your projects may be slightly different, but the principle is the same. Ensure that you are not spending your homework time trying to get all your project done on one night. Plan it out, spread it out – it will be easier and you will get a better result.

**Study for Exams**
The final thing you should do during your homework time is prepare for your exams. Unlike what many students think, exam preparation should begin at the beginning of the year – not towards the end. We'll discuss exams in more detail later but following are some basic ideas. We talked about how memory works

earlier and that is very relevant when we consider exams. Think about it – exams test your knowledge from earlier in the year so the more you remember the better you will do. The key is to transfer as much information from short to long-term memory as you can. This means that you need to begin remembering information as soon as you learn it – that's what the class revision is for.

The best way to prepare for exams is to create exam study cards. For these you can use index cards or library catalogue cards which can be purchased at stationery shops. The process is as follows:

Firstly, examine the summaries you created of the day's class notes – look for important ideas, key principles and significant facts. How do you know if something is important, key or significant? For this you will need to know what the topic is, listen to suggestions from the teacher ("remember this, class" or "this is important, class"), and note how the textbook organises information – items like chapter titles, and section headings should give you an indication of important ideas.

Once you have identified the important ideas, key principles and significant facts you need to ensure that you understand them (*NOTE: there is no point remembering something that you do not understand, so with all of this I am assuming you understand everything in your notes – if you don't, refer to the section about asking questions*). Once you understand them you need to write them down onto the cards.

But simply writing them onto the cards will not suffice – you must write them in a way that will make them easier to remember. One of the best ways is with numbered lists. A numbered list helps you to prioritise and remember ideas, and makes summarising very easy. For example, numbered lists could include: The 7 Causes of World War One; The 4 Properties of Electricity; The 5 Pillars of Islam; The 3 Types of Shakespeare Plays; and the list goes on – there is almost no information that cannot be turned into a numbered list.

So, your study card will contain a very clear title of the topic (easy to see and remember) and a numbered list which can be read and recited quickly and easily. Using colours to highlight key ideas will help, but ensure your cards are still clear and easy to read. Number your cards according to when they were created – that way you know their order.

The final step is to keep your study cards with you (in your pocket or your bag) and read them whenever you have a chance: a few minutes in class after your work has been completed, whilst you are waiting for the bus, mute the TV while the ads are on, any time – even a few seconds to glance at a few of the cards will embed them into your memory. When you step into that exam at the end of the semester or year you can be confident of knowing the information that you need.

**You have No Homework?**
I've lost count of the number of times I've had parents say to me: "Every night when I ask my son/daughter if they have any homework, they always tell me they have none." It is an unfortunately common occurrence. Students all over the world are telling their parents that they don't have any homework – either because they don't want to do any (they are lying) or they don't know what more they can do (they are disorganised). Now, you are in neither position.

As soon as you have read this section you will never be able to say: "I have no homework." If you have no classwork to complete or revise, you have completed all your assignments and studied adequately for all your exams there is still plenty that you can do. If it's not the end of the year there is plenty of reading that you can do to expand your knowledge and increase your understanding of current topics – there is no end to the amount of reading that can be done! If it is the end of the year there is always plenty of preparation that can be done for next year.

Someone who wants to be successful at high school should never say that they have no homework – there is always something that can be done. Improve, expand, and explore – there is always something else to learn!

## Study Sessions

Now that you know what the different types of homework are it is important to organise your study sessions so that you can maximise your effectiveness and efficiency. There are a few key principles to keep in mind when you are planning your homework time.

### Plan

Firstly, ensure that you plan your time use in advance. Do not wait until you are sitting at your desk, ready to begin working, before you think about what you are doing. All your activities should be planned – and the more carefully you plan the quicker you will complete the work and the better it will be. Ideally you should set aside a few minutes (it shouldn't take more than a few minutes to plan an evening's homework) at the beginning of each study session to plan what you will be doing during it. Because of your study timetable you know what subject you will be working on, but what specifically will you be doing?

- Do you have any unfinished work to complete?
- Do you have many class notes to rewrite and summarise?
- Are there any ideas/concepts that were discussed in class that you did not understand? Do you need to do a bit more reading?
- What assignments are you currently working on? Which of them are the highest priority (refer to your goals)?
- Do you have some important ideas, key principles or significant facts that need to be placed on study cards for future revision?

Once you have determined the answers to these questions, you can plan your time so that you are working through each of the items that needs to be done. Approximate how much time you will need to complete each task and try to stick to that time. For example, if you give yourself 25 minutes to work on an English essay do it for 25 minutes and then stop. If you don't, you risk using up all your time and not having enough time for other tasks. If you have planned your work wisely you will have multiple days to complete larger tasks and you don't need to get it all done on one night.

*NOTE: at first, it may be difficult to approximate how much time your tasks will take, sometimes you will give yourself too much time, sometimes not enough. Don't worry, the more to do it the more accurate you will become.*

Also remember that some nights you will not have incomplete work or notes to revise, so you can focus on completing assignments; other nights you may have some work to complete but no study cards to prepare. By planning each night in advance you will not waste time or miss something that needs to be done.

### Session Length

There is some disagreement regarding the ideal length of study sessions. Some people advise short sessions to maximise energy and add variety, others determine that longer sessions are better because they make use of momentum to increase your efficiency. Let's look at the advantages and disadvantages of both so that you can make up your own mind.

Short study sessions are normally 30-45 minutes (anything shorter does not allow much time for quality work) and have a few advantages. These include:

- Reducing boredom because of the relatively rapid changes;
- Enabling a variety of subjects to be studied in one night;
- Enabling flexibility in your schedule – you do not need large blocks of time;

However, short study sessions also have some disadvantages, including:

- Not enough time to develop deep thinking if you have heavy problem solving to do;
- Generally, require stronger self-discipline to maintain and organise;
- You are unable to use momentum to achieve more;

Longer study sessions are usually 1 to 1½ hours (anything longer and you become less efficient) and also have both advantages and disadvantages. The advantages include:

- Time to develop deep thinking and complex problem solving;
- Easier to organise and maintain;
- Able to use your momentum to achieve more;

The disadvantages of longer study times include:

- Less variety of subjects to be studied in one night;

- Large blocks of time are needed;
- Can lose focus due to boredom or fatigue;

As you can see there is good and bad with each option – which one is better for you is something that only you can decide. Try both long and short study sessions to see which ones you prefer. Which one you choose will determine how your daily program and study timetable looks. You will either have a few long sessions, or many shorter ones each night.

### Regular Breaks

When organising your study it is vital that you build in regular study breaks. The main reason for this is to keep your brain fresh – like any part of the body, your brain, if it is used constantly will tire, and a tired brain will result in reduced effectiveness. Just like your brain needs rest each day (sleep) it also needs regular rests during the day – and although it would be nice, I do not mean regular naps. Regular rest means small breaks on a regular basis.

I like working on a guide of 10% for breaks, meaning 10% of your study sessions should be a break. So, if your study session is 30 minutes, three minutes of that would be a break, or if your session was 60 minutes your break would be six minutes of that time. This is just a rough guide but it's easy to calculate and it provides a good study to break ratio. That means that if you are doing three hours of study approximately 20 minutes of that would be taken in breaks – six minutes out of every hour.

Don't give in to the temptation to miss your study break! You are motivated to complete your work, you feel good and 'you're on a roll' – the temptation to miss the break and just keep on working may be strong, but don't. Remember, a brain without rest becomes less effective so regular breaks will keep you at your best.

### Different Activities During Breaks

It's not only important that you take regular breaks when you are studying, but also to plan what you do during your breaks. To be effective your break must be an activity which is different to the activity you were doing when you were studying. That means that if you were sitting down and writing during your study you should do something where you are not sitting down and not writing in your break. If you are reading during your study you should not read during your break. If you were working on a screen (computer or tablet) for your study you should not use one during your break.

Do something very different during your break – preferably something that's going to refresh you and enliven you for the next study session. The best examples include:

- get some exercise – this doesn't mean you must run a marathon between every study session, a simple walk up and down the yard may suffice;
- do some chores around the house – this is a good way to get chores done and get a break at the same time, plus they don't usually take that long;
- take a shower – maybe not 'every' break, but it could be an opportunity to get cleaned and refreshed, plus the shower is a great way to promote creativity;
- grab a snack – the simple process of walking to the kitchen or fridge may be enough to refresh you, just make sure your snack is not junk food;
- talk to your family – a couple of minutes to catch-up with parents could be all the break you need, plus it will show them that you are serious about your study;
- play with your dog – exercise, excitement, enthusiasm and lots of fun, and it will be good for you, too;

These are just some examples of what your breaks could look like, but they are all different from what you were doing during your study session. When you conduct your breaks like this you will find that they refresh you, and when you return to your study you will be more alert and ready to tackle your next task.

- *ACTION – create 'break cards'. Produce a series of cards (15-20 is a good number) and on each one place an activity that can be done during a break – remember what makes a break effective. Shuffle the cards and when it's time for a break pick up the top card and that's what you are doing for your break. This adds variety and a bit of excitement to your breaks.*

## Prioritising

We've already looked at the importance of prioritising goals/tasks, and that is vital with homework. Each task must be prioritised before you begin – start with the most important one first. But what makes one task more important than another? Don't make the mistake of judging task importance just by how much an assignment is worth to your grades – there's more to it than that. Consider how much time you have to complete each task, what each task is going to contribute to your overall learning, how much each particular task is going to take and how difficult it is.

Let's look at some examples: you have unfinished work from today's history class; notes from a new topic in Science; a major project for technology due in five weeks; a Geography test in one week to study for; and a major essay for English due in two weeks. Your unfinished History work is important because you cannot allow gaps to develop in your learning and understanding, and you need to commit the information to your long-term memory; your Science notes are important because you must commit the new information to your long-term memory; your major Technology project is important because it is worth a lot to your grades, but you have five weeks so you can spread out the work; study for your Geography test is important but you don't have to do it all in one night – you can spread it out over the next week; and your English essay is important because it's English and it's worth a lot – but you have two weeks to finish it. Based in this information I would prioritise and plan the study session's tasks as follows:

1. Finish work from History class (10 min);
2. Rewrite notes for new topic from Science class (10 min);
3. Work on Technology project (20 min);
4. Study for Geography test (20 min);
5. Work on English essay (20 min);

Once again, this is just an example but it shows how you can prioritise your tasks to ensure that you are spreading your time wisely.

## Regular Reviews

We have talked about regular reviews before, and how much difference they can make to your success. Integrate regular reviews into your study sessions – they don't need to take up a lot of time but they can save you a lot of time. Set aside a five-minute block each day to review that day, set aside a 10-minute block each week to review that week, set aside an hour each term to review that term, and set aside a whole day to review each year. You will find that you will not miss the time you spent on reviewing but you will notice how much more productive and effective you are when regular reviews are a habit.

## Using a Planner

We talked about how important it is to develop the use of a planner into a habit – that planner is vital for successful study sessions. The planner should be used, during and after classes, to record everything that needs to be done, such as unfinished class work, homework given in class, major and minor tasks, and upcoming tests and exams. It should also be used to record due dates for assessments and tasks.

When your study session begins, the planner should be used to plan and prioritise tasks for the session – it should be an integral part of the planning process. The planner can also be used to record things that need to be done (such as asking the teacher a question) during the next school day.

## Group Work

In the final part of this section we will discuss how to use group work to study successfully. Sometimes you may have the opportunity to share your study with other people and you should take it – there are many advantages with group work, if it is just a small part of your total study sessions.

It is said that 'two heads are better than one' and this can be true studying in groups. With the right group, you can use group work to your advantage. Here are some of the benefits: share the workload; motivate each other; keep each other accountable; keep each other focused; others may have strengths that you don't; and it can make study fun.

## Choose your Group Carefully

Firstly, it's important to choose the right study group – don't just agree to join anyone for regular study sessions. A study group that will help you to be successful is one that wants the same thing that you do – success. Choose people who are motivated, focused and willing to do their best, not because they are popular, good-looking, rich, or any other non-success-related reason.

## Choose a Leader

It's also important to choose a leader of the group. The leader must be willing to organise the group and ensure that the sessions run smoothly. A study group leader is not someone who tells others in the group what they must do, but rather someone who is able to motivate the members of the group, plan the study sessions and co-ordinate contacts between members. If you are organising the group then you could try being the leader – it will be great experience for you, or you can rotate the leadership throughout the group.

## Expectations and Rules

One of the first tasks of the group is to agree to expectations and rules. Without these a group can quickly turn into a disorganised mess which is not helpful to anyone. Some examples of expectations and rules include:

- Everyone takes a turn at hosting the group;
- The host provides drinks and snacks;
- Everyone must bring their own equipment;
- Only members of the group can attend, unless the group agrees to a visitor;
- The session doesn't go longer than two hours;

These must be agreed to by the entire group before they can be adopted. Once they have been adopted they should be written down and distributed to all members of the group.

### Summarise the Task

Before you can effectively work together as a group you must all have a clear understanding of the task. Talk about this as a group. Ask questions if there is any part of the task that is not clear. Discuss all the parts of the task. Clarify the due date, the marking criteria (if you have them) and anything that the teacher has said about the task in class.

Once you all have a clearer understanding of the task you should each write a summary of the task in your own words. Then share your summaries as a group and compare any differences. This will confirm or deny that everyone has a clear understanding of what the group will be working on.

## Determine Goals and Responsibilities

When the task is clear, it is time to determine the goals of the group. Is the goal to complete one task, such as an assignment, after which it will disband? Or is the goal to improve everyone's understanding and performance through the year in a particular subject? The goal may be a combination of these or something very different. Whatever the goal or goals of the group it is vital that they are discussed and clarified the first time that the group meets, and every time a new person joins. Failure to clarify goals will lead to some members of the group becoming unhappy with the direction of the group or its results.

It is also important to determine what everyone's responsibilities are from the outset. Is one person going to be the group contact? Will someone keep all the work that is completed by the group? Will someone be the person who asks the teacher questions that have been discussed by the group? These and any other responsibilities may be important to the smooth running of the group and it's vital that everyone knows who is responsible for what, before work starts.

## Share Work Based on Skills and Experience

One of the potential problems with group work is that not all the members are equal – some write well, others draw well, others are good speakers – this can lead to some members of the team doing more of the work than others. Firstly, let me say that inequality is not always a bad thing – if it is based on skills and talents. If some people are good writers then others may not be equal to them when it comes to writing, or if some people are good speakers then others may not be equal to them when it comes to speaking. In this sense equality is used as a measure of skill and ability, not personal worth – with personal worth, all people are equal!

Secondly, let me say that if you are one of the people who is always doing more of the work, then well done! Embrace it, rather than complaining about it. Think about this – you learn by doing, so the more you do the more you learn. That means that those people in the group who are doing all the work are getting a better education, and those people who are sitting back and letting you do all the work are wasting their own time. They may think that they are smart to let others do their work, but the opposite is true.

Thirdly, I would say that you should make it a policy of your study group to distribute the tasks according to what each person's strengths are. Let the good writers do the writing, let the good researchers do the research, etc. Everyone can develop these skills in their individual class work, but in group work you should focus on your strengths.

**Determine Meeting Times and Regularity**
The final factor to organise is timing – this means how often you meet and how long meetings last. This should be agreed upon during the first meeting so that all group members know what to expect. Ultimately, the regularity of group study sessions depends upon the needs and schedules of the group members, and the requirements of the task or tasks. For example, if the task is a major assignment due in five weeks then group sessions will have to be planned to allow enough time to co-ordinate tasks. If one of the group members has sports practise every Wednesday night then the group will have to meet on alternative nights. You get the idea.

The other thing to consider is how long will each meeting take – one hour, six hours, or something in between? Once again this depends upon the task and the group. If you are meeting only once every two weeks then a longer study session may be better, but if you are meeting every other day then a smaller session would be preferable. Either way, ensure that all members of the group agree to the schedule and any changes that are made. This will ensure that the study group helps all its members be successful.

## Homework Action Plan

1. Make a list of possible activities that you can do during study breaks. Try to add variety so that the breaks energise you.
2. Make a list of people who would be good to have in a study group. Approach each of them to see if they would be interested.

# Part 8 – Notes

### *He listens well who takes notes*

*Dante Alighieri*

The ability to take effective notes is a skill that will benefit you well beyond high school. It will be necessary at university and when you get a job, so developing the skill now is a good idea. Effective note-taking is seen either as unimportant or as a secret skill which is too difficult to learn – neither of those positions is correct: taking effective notes is simply a matter of being organised, planning and consciously thinking about your own learning. Let's look at some ideas about note-taking that can be easily put into practice.

## Taking Notes

Before we look at 'how' to take effective notes, let's spend a moment talking about 'why' taking notes is important. Basically, the reason we need to take notes, in school or at work, is either because we forget stuff, or we remember too much stuff! Whenever we receive a lot of information (such as during class) we are constantly being bombarded with multiple inputs: the teacher speaking, students around us talking, sounds of paper shuffling or noises from the hallway, the smells of your class mates (some good, some bad, ewww!), your rumbling stomach, thoughts of the test you have next period, and many more distractions. Through all this you can miss what's important. By writing down things that the teacher says, or from the textbook, or PowerPoint slides, or however your teacher communicates with you during class you will be able to keep the main ideas to be digested later. Without notes, any information that was gathered during the class will quickly fade away as soon as the bell goes.

Another important factor to remember is the physiological reasons for note-taking. When you are involved in the physical act of writing something down a particular process takes place in your nervous system – let's look at it: the information comes to you either as light into your eyes (you see it) or as sound into your ears (you hear it); once the input reaches your brain it is processed into words and ideas that you can understand; your brain then sends signals to your hand to write that information down; as each word or idea is written down it is acknowledged by the brain which reprocesses it. This process, which in reality takes microseconds, creates a feedback loop between your brain and your hand which reinforces the information that is being written down. This makes it easier to process and remember. Unfortunately, the process does not work the same way when you are typing information (due to the disconnect between keyboard and screen) that is why hand-writing notes is much more effective.

## Be Prepared

The first rule of effective note-taking is to always be prepared. Always have your note-taking equipment ready at hand (pads of paper, pens, rulers, etc.) even if there's not much chance of notes during a particular class. You don't know when you will need to take some important notes – and it will usually be when you don't have your equipment with you.

## Don't Borrow from Others

Although it may be tempting at times, don't borrow notes from other people. This isn't because I think it's cheating, or something like that, but because notes written by other people will not be as useful for you. A person writes notes based upon what they feel is important and in a manner that makes sense to them. Besides that, the very process of writing notes helps you to understand and remember the information more effectively. If you rely on the notes of others you will be making your own learning more difficult.

The only exception to this is if you are absent from a class and you missed the opportunity to take your own notes. In that case, find someone who writes similar notes to you, who also wants success like you do, and borrow their notes. However, don't just copy them down, word for word – read them, ensure you understand them and write your own notes from them – just as if you were taking notes from a textbook. Also, ask them if there is something in the notes that you do not understand – this will help both of you.

## Be Clear and Neat

Your notes need to be easy for you to read – now and in the future. Having notes that need to be carefully deciphered later to be understood is a waste of time and energy. I've known students who have kept their notes as loose scraps of paper in their lockers – needless to say, they were not successful at school.

Ensure that your notes are carefully and neatly written so that anyone could read them without needing an interpreter. If you have terrible handwriting (like me) and even your neatest effort comes out looking like scratches made by a chicken then you need to spend some time rewriting (or even typing) them at home. Trust me, you will be grateful for neat notes when it's exam time.

## Organise your Notes

It is very important to ensure that your notes are organised in a way that makes them easy to store and find later. Someone who keeps their notes as scraps of paper in their locker is going to have difficulty finding their notes for a topic if they need to. Your level of organisation should be so precise that you can find a particular sentence out of a year's worth of notes if you need to. Try these strategies to organise your notes:

- Use headings and titles to indicate topics or subtopics. You can have multiple headings and subheadings (indicated by font size, indentation, underlining or colours). This makes finding a topic easy.

- Use numbering or dates for every page of your notes. You can number your notes (first page 1, second page 2, etc.) or add the dates that the notes are taken on the top of the page to make identifying chronological order easier.

- Use folders to store your notes when they are completed. Manila folders or loose leaf binders organised into subject areas can keep your notes organised and easy to access. Transfer your notes into your folders as you complete them and you will always have a clear record. If you are eager you can scan your notes and have digital copies – that would be impressive!

- Use dividers in your folders to break up subjects into topic areas. For example, Science could be broken up into Electricity, Magnetism, Chemistry, etc.

## Use Lists

We've already looked at the benefits of lists and how they can make you more effective (see Part 4 – Habits). This is also the case with your notes. Using lists to simplify and summarise your notes can make them quicker to write and easier to remember. Compare these two examples:

*The techniques used to persuade with language include: exaggeration, facts and statistics, connotation, emotive language, appeals to fear, appeals to patriotism, tone, and expert opinion.*

*Techniques of language persuasion:*
- *Exaggeration;*
- *Facts and statistics;*
- *Connotation;*
- *Emotive language;*
- *Appeals to fear;*
- *Appeals to patriotism;*

- *Tone;*
- *Expert opinion;*

Of the two examples above, which would be easier to remember? The list is quicker to read and easier to remember and can be placed onto a study card for quick reference when studying for an exam. It can also be rearranged into a mnemonic for even easier recall. Use lists as much as possible when writing notes and you will find your notes are a lot more useful.

### Use Abbreviations or Shorthand Codes

Another way to make your notes more effective is to use abbreviations or shorthand. These will enable you to write your notes much quicker and will ensure that you don't miss anything. Abbreviations are any shortened words you use to represent other words, and shorthand is a language of symbols used to represent words or phrases. Shorthand is a language that is not used much anymore but you don't need to learn it to improve the rapidity of your note-taking.

It is very simple to develop your own system of abbreviations and shorthand – for abbreviations simply shorten the word in a way that it is still recognisable, for shorthand just use or invent any symbol that can be used instead of the word or phrase. Some suggestions are below:

| Suggested Abbreviations | | Suggested Shorthand Symbols | |
|---|---|---|---|
| because = b/c | language = lang | and = & | example = eg |
| review = rvw | examination = exm | good = ☺ | this leads to = → |

The extent of abbreviations and shorthand that you use is totally up to you. It may be something that you develop with your study group, or you can keep it to yourself. At first it will seem silly and difficult to remember, but as you get into the habit of using it (particularly some abbreviations or symbols) you will find that they come naturally to you and effective note-taking has become second nature.

**Look Out for Repetition**

To ensure that you include the most important information into your notes it is vital that you listen for repetitions from the teacher. If there is particular information which the teacher is repeating throughout the class then you can assume that the information is important. Even if it is not important, the fact that the teacher repeats it suggests that they think it is important and so it will probably be a good idea to remember it for later use.

### Listen for Signals

A simple cue from teachers that something important is about to be shared may include phrases such as "this is important", "take note of this", "remember this", or "this will be in the exam." Any of these (or similar cues) are signals from the teacher to write it down. Take note of these cues and anything that follows them and you will not miss what counts.

Another cue from the teacher to listen for is signals that lists are coming up. As we've already determined, a list is the ideal tool for note-taking so when you can, write your list directly into your notes. Signals such as "the first reason is…", or "there are six reasons for…", or "there are several factors which…", or anything else which indicates that a list of items is soon to follow.

## Reviewing Notes

Writing notes in class is not the only important part of effective note-taking – it's only the first part. Once your notes have been written it is important to review them a few times to ensure they have been understood, absorbed and remembered.

### Rewriting Notes

The first part of reviewing your notes is rewriting them. This may seem like a waste of time but it's not. Notes that are written in class are generally messy and imprecise due to the classroom environment which contains distractions and pressure. By rewriting your notes, you will be able to clarify thoughts and ideas and express them in a much clearer way. You will also be able to add or subtract thoughts and ideas to make your notes clearer and more effective.

### Rereading Notes

Once you have rewritten your notes you must reread them to let your mind absorb them. Do this multiple times, a few times aloud if possible, for maximum impact. When you have started to absorb the information, you can begin to produce study cards from your notes (see Types of Homework in Part 7 – Homework).

## Notes Action Plan

1. Prepare your note-taking equipment in advance. Purchase a note pad and pens which can be your regular 'note-taking kit'.
2. Consider which words you regularly use can be abbreviated, and which words or phrases can be turned into shorthand symbols. Create a list of them.

# Part 9 – Reading

*Reading is to the mind what exercise is to the body.*

*Joseph Addison*

As we discussed previously, reading is one of the most important habits you can form to increase your success – not just at high school but in life. Reading will make you smarter and will enable you to achieve more and get better results. It sounds like magic, doesn't it? Trust me, reading can be! Let's look at some ways to get the most out of your reading.

## SQ3R

The SQ3R method of reading has been around for many years and is a useful strategy to adopt for comprehensive understanding. It stands for the five steps of effective reading: survey, question, read, recite, review. Each of these steps leads to a deeper understanding of the book.

*NOTE: although this method could be used on any books it is designed primarily for non-fiction books that are read for learning, not enjoyment.*

## Survey

The first step is to survey the book. Don't begin reading the book but instead examine the various elements of it to learn how the book is structured.

- Look at the cover – what information does it give you about the content of the book;
- Examine the table of contents – how is the book structured;
- Inspect chapter and section headings and internal sub-headings – how are ideas developed in the book;
- Look at maps, photos or other graphics throughout the book;
- Does it have an index? – if so, what key words or concepts can you find;

A survey does not have to be detailed or lengthy – it can be done effectively in a few minutes – but it will give you an overall 'feel' for the book and enable your reading or study to be more effective.

## Question

The next step is to ask questions about the book before you start reading. This can be done at the Survey stage. Ask questions about the book, the author or the publisher such as:

- What does the main purpose of the book seem to be?
- What other books is the author known for?
- What type of books does the publisher make?

Ask questions relating to yourself, such as:

- How much do I know about this topic?
- How interested am I in this topic?
- Is this book at my most comfortable level of reading?

Asking these and many other related questions will encourage you to contemplate the subject matter before you start reading. Once again, the process doesn't need to take a long time, and it doesn't need to be written down, but it will give you some context before you start reading.

**Read**

The next step is the most obvious, but often the most misunderstood. Reading a book (unless you are reading a novel for pleasure) is about learning and understanding, and it is one of the easiest and best ways to do so. Too many students look at reading as if it is a trial or a punishment, but it should be looked at as an opportunity. As someone who wants to be successful you should always be eager to do some reading.

As you read, consider the thoughts you had and the questions you asked earlier. Think about the main idea of the book and how it is developed. When you get to the end of a chapter or section stop and consider what you have just read. Summarise the ideas of that chapter in your mind. Consider what new things you have learned.

Continue to read until you have read the entire book – it doesn't have to be in one sitting but that does have some advantages.

**Recite**

After you have read through the book you must go back and begin to explore the book in more depth. As you continue reading use a pen or pencil (assuming the book is yours) to mark words, phrases or passages that pique your interest. Jot down notes as they come to you and questions that can be answered later.

When you encounter a word that you don't know stop and define the word using a dictionary – it may even be an idea to create a list of new words to learn. When you read a passage that is difficult to understand reread it and think about it until you do understand it. Remember, you don't want to have gaps in your knowledge.

**Review**

The final step is review what you have read – that is, read it again, maybe not completely but at least to reinforce the main ideas to yourself. Reread the notes that you added to the book, the things you underlined or highlighted and the questions you asked.

It is best to review the book a couple of days after you read it. This allows your mind to absorb the ideas and come up with more questions. Ideally, you should review the book multiple times, each with at least a few days between reviews. This will help you to get a deeper understanding of the book and what it is trying to share with you. The time that you invest in this process will be paid back in deeper understanding and more diverse knowledge.

## Speed Reading

Speed reading is a skill that enables you to read a lot of information in a short amount of time. Experienced speed readers can read hundreds of pages an hour and thus, multiple books a week. It makes studying and research much more effective and can be very beneficial to a person's success.

Speed reading is basically a process involving skimming the words on the page to pick-up key words and ideas, and when it is done correctly, the main ideas of a paragraph can be collected without having to spend time reading every word in the paragraph. Speed reading is not recommended for casual reading, because it does take more energy, although if you become adept at speed reading for study you will find that your casual reading becomes faster, too.

To learn how to develop speed reading there are many books that can teach it and there are classes that can be taken. These are generally short and inexpensive but will be well worth the investment. It is possibly something that can be done over the summer in preparation for beginning the school year.

- *ACTION – conduct an Internet search of the speed reading courses in your area. Look at costs, availability and length. If you are able examine reviews of the courses so that you can choose the most effective one. Once you have the best one call the organisers and make a booking.*

## Context

Another important procedure for getting the most out of books is exploring context. Context is the background, historical, cultural and social information that is not mentioned in the book but may be relevant to a greater understanding of its subject matter. For example, if I am reading a book on Nelson Mandela then I may want to explore the history of South Africa, the development of Apartheid, African music and literature and the tribal divisions of Africa. Although these may not be directly related to the story of Nelson Mandela, understanding them will give you a much deeper understanding of the man and the historical character.

Exploring context can involve a lot of extra reading, but it doesn't have to. Websites like Wikipedia can provide basic contextual information in short articles – and they don't usually cost anything.

## Repetition

A basic principle that is vital to a deeper understanding of the books you read is repetition. The truth is that the more you read something the more you will remember about it and the better you will understand it. Each time you read something you will pick-up some of the meanings and ideas in it but not all of them. The next time you read it you will understand more, the third time even more, and so on.

I've seen this taking place in my own reading. Two things that I read repeatedly are the Bible and the plays of William Shakespeare. I have read these multiple times over the last 30+ years and I've found that each time I read them I discover something new – something that I haven't noticed – even though I've read that same passage or page many times before. This never fails to work. Just when I think I've fully understood a book of the Bible or play of Shakespeare they will surprise me, and I'll learn even more.

Of course, this doesn't work with all books. Some books are very simple and do not have multiple layers of meaning, and that's okay – sometimes you just want to read about 'the cow jumping over the moon', but when you want to explore a book, to dig into it and extract as many ideas, thoughts, themes as you can then you must read it more than just once.

This may seem like a waste of time, but it's not – it's an investment. Just like with everything that we are discussing in this book success involves doing extra, going further, and repeat reading is a big part of that. Try it and see how much of a difference it makes to your understanding of a book.

*NOTE: as mentioned right at the beginning, you should read this book multiple times to get the most out of it, too.*

## Annotating

Annotating simply means writing notes in the book you are reading. As I've mentioned several times throughout this book, writing down ideas and thoughts is an important way to help your brain process what you have learned. Doing it while you read is an important step in getting the most out of your reading.

To annotate effectively ensure you have a pen or pencil handy and that the book is yours and can be written in – if it's not you may need to write your notes on a piece of paper, which is not as good, but is better than nothing. When you annotate, you are using your pen to indicate anything that is interesting or worth remembering. Underline phrases that are important or memorable, circle key or unfamiliar words, jot down questions, ideas or thoughts that come up when you are reading, use arrows to link similar ideas or brackets to group them.

An effectively annotated book should have writing and underlining all over it – making it a more valuable resource than the book alone. In fact, when I used to teach literature I would expect my students to annotate their texts extensively, and those who did usually had a much better understanding of it.

The process of annotating a book takes your brain to a deeper level of processing and helps you understand the book better. It also gives you extra material to examine when you are rereading – you never know what new ideas will be prompted by the extra notes.

## Reading Aloud

Another important idea on reading is reading aloud. This is usually seen as something that is done with small children, not older ones, but there are many distinct advantages to reading aloud and it should be a part of your reading repertoire. Reading aloud works because it gives your brain a different input with which to process your reading. Usually we read with our eyes only, which is okay, but it's one input only. When we read aloud we use our eyes and our ears – that doubles the input that our brain is getting and leads to better understanding and memorisation.

This 'double input' helps us pick up ideas more effectively, process ideas quicker and hear the flow of the words – giving you a greater appreciation of the language. This is particularly useful when you are reading something that is unfamiliar or difficult to understand. A difficult passage becomes easier when it is read aloud.

Of course, there are certain circumstances when reading aloud does not work – in a library, for example. You must have a quiet place where there are no distractions and no audience, reading quietly in your room or outside when there is no one around is best. It doesn't have to be loud, either. Because you are only reading to yourself you only need to read loudly enough to understand yourself. You will find that reading aloud does make a difference to your understanding of the books you read and will become a useful tool leading to greater success.

## Levels of Reading

I've spent a lot of time telling you how important reading is to success in high school. Without reading you will not be successful – but with reading there can be different levels of success. Two students can both read lots but receive very different benefits from reading. This is because reading can be done in more depth or less. Let's look at the different levels of reading:

1. The basic level of reading is that you read only those things that you are required to read and nothing else – this will help you to achieve passing grades and will probably place you in the top half of your class. For example, you read the Shakespeare play 'Hamlet';

2. The intermediate level of reading is that in addition to reading what you are required to read you also read a range of books relating to those books. This will place you in the top 10% of the class. For example, you read 'Hamlet' but also a few books discussing 'Hamlet' and some general books on Shakespeare;

3. The advanced level of reading is that in addition to the above (the basic and intermediate reading) you also read a wide range of books on personal development. This includes books about organisation, time management, attitude, goals and healthy habits. These books are not directly related to the above reading but will make you more effective and more successful, not just at school but for life.

The bottom line is that you should be reading as much as possible – an hour a day or more – if you really want to be successful, and that doesn't include reading for pleasure. Adequate time for reading should be built into your daily schedule and made into a habit. If you are reading a variety of books you will find that all aspects of your life will improve and your capabilities will continually expand. If you focus your reading in a particular area (such as where you want your career to be when you finish school) you will find that before too long you will become an expert in the field. Reading can be that effective!

## Reading Action Plan

1. Spend some time now researching speed reading options in your area. Are there some inexpensive books available? Are there any speed reading workshops taking place nearby?

2. Create a Personal Reading List of books that you want to read and begin working your way through it – right now. Commit to reading at least one of them every month.

# Part 10 – Writing Essays

*The art of writing is the art of discovering what you believe.*

*Gustave Flaubert*

Writing essays is a large and important part of high school (especially at the top end) and you must learn to do it well if you wish to be successful. Writing essays can seem to be an intimidating exercise for most students, but it doesn't have to be so. With the right approach and adequate planning, writing an essay can be a relatively straightforward and simple process. In the following section, we will look at some important principles to remember when writing essays, how to plan them and the best way to write them.

## Important Principles of Essay Writing

Some people may think it strange to be talking about principles of essay writing – aren't essays just pieces of writing? Don't you just sit down and start writing until you are finished? Not if you want to be successful! As we have already discussed many times in this book you cannot complete any task without planning it. This is more applicable with essays because they can be complicated, and difficult to complete without planning and organisation. So, let's look at some of these principles before we deal with the planning and organisation of your essays.

## Analyse the Question

One of the first (and most important) principles of successful essay writing is analysing the question. If you do not analyse the question you will not know what you are being asked to do – if you do not know what you are being asked to do you will certainly not be able to achieve it adequately. Too many students read the question quickly, and then begin writing their answer to it without really knowing exactly what it is asking.

Essay questions may seem straight forward but that is not necessarily the case. Essay questions often have multiple parts and can ask you to address different aspects of a topic. If you fail to read these questions carefully you risk missing important parts and providing an incomplete answer. To analyse an essay question ask yourself the following:

- Does this question have more than one part?
- Does this question address multiple aspects of the topic?
- What key words (such as compare, contrast, discuss, analyse) does the question contain?

- If I were to rewrite the question in my own words (without changing the meaning) what would it become?

Once you have read and analysed the question you will have a better idea of what is expected of you, and thus your chances of providing what is expected are much higher.

### Planning

The second important step in the writing of an essay is the planning stage. If you plan your essay well the rest of it will be simpler and better, but if you don't plan you will struggle for coherence and clarity.

*NOTE: You will see these two words a lot in this part of the book: coherence and clarity. Coherence is the unity of the essay – the ideas match the thesis (main idea) of the essay and follow a logical order. Without coherence, an essay will look disorganised and 'stuck together'. Clarity is how clear the ideas are to follow and understand. An essay which has clarity has ideas and arguments which are easy to understand, but an essay without clarity leaves the reader wondering what they have just read.*

The first stage of planning is the brainstorming. This is where you sit down with a pen and piece of paper, and for a few minutes write down everything that comes into your mind about the question/topic. It doesn't matter if the ideas are right, wrong, big, small, silly or serious – just write them down! Any idea that comes into your mind should be written down. At the end of a few minutes you should have at least a page of messy, disorganised ideas.

*NOTE: it is best if these steps are not completed directly one after the other. Having some time between them allows your brain to process ideas and thoughts. Try leaving at least a day between these steps.*

Next, filter the ideas that you have just written. Read each idea – is it relevant? Is it correct? Does it answer the question? Ignore all those points which are not relevant, not correct and do not answer the question, and copy the rest onto another piece of paper. You should now have a list of ideas which have some relevance to the question.

Now, read through your list and organise the ideas according to their relevance to the question. You should be left with a list of clear ideas which can be used in your essay. When you start the writing process you will already have your ideas ready to be used. They will probably need to be adjusted and modified but that will come later.

## Multiple Drafts

Another important principle of essay writing is multiple drafts. By this I mean writing a first draft, a second draft, a third draft, etc. Too many students believe that when they have written their essay the first time, it is finished, but that should not be the case. The first draft of any document, be it a letter, a novel or an essay, still has much room for improvement. If it is submitted at that time it is not as good as it could be – and as someone who wants to be successful in high school, you should be wanting it to be as good as possible.

If you follow the process I set down, your first draft will be rough and needing much revision. That is because your first draft should be written for completion, not polish. Each time you rewrite your essay it improves, especially if others check it. So, the more drafts you write, the more improvements it will have. Obviously, there are limits to how many drafts you can produce – time is limited and a point is reached when draft improvements are not worth the time invested. This point is usually reached around 3-4 drafts.

## Multiple Revisions

Another important principle for a successful essay is multiple revisions – or ensuring the draft is checked before starting on the next draft. It is the nature of writing that when you read something you have written previously you will read it with slightly different eyes. Think about when you read something you wrote when you were a young child – you know it was you writing but it's sounds childish and silly – like someone else wrote it. This can work to your advantage with essay writing. Write it, leave it for a while and then when you reread (especially if you read it with an 'eye' for improvement) it you will see multiple ways that it can be improved.

This works best when a significant amount of time has passed. For example, if you reread something as soon as you finish writing it you may pick up a few errors, but if you leave it for a few days and then reread it your mind will be fresh and your revision will be much more effective. That is why it is important to plan to complete your writing well before the due date – to give yourself time to make improvements.

An even better way to revise your drafts is to have someone else read it. Teachers are the best option, because they know what to look for, but they are busy and will probably not have time to check your drafts. Alternatives include, parents, older siblings or other family members, neighbours, tutors or other adults who have both the time and the willingness to help you out.

For this to work you need to ensure that the person reading your draft knows what is expected in an essay (asking Uncle George, who has not seen an essay in his life, may not be helpful), and that they will be honest with their criticism (asking Great Aunt Mary, may not work because she thinks everything you do is perfect already).

At the very least, asking someone else to read a draft will help you improve the flow and clarity of the writing – they will be able to tell you if sentences do not make sense and that what you have written is clear and logical. Having a different person check different drafts can also be a good idea. For example, Dad checks Draft 1, Uncle Jimmy checks Draft 2, and Coach Harden checks Draft 3. If you improve your essay after each draft, by the time you submit it to your teacher it will be so much better than if you didn't draft at all. It may take a little longer but success doesn't happen overnight.

### Right or Wrong – Follow the Evidence

I have spent much time trying to convince students that there are no right or wrong answers in essays. Although there are a few exceptions, essays are about your opinion, and your opinion cannot be wrong – **IF** you can support it with evidence. That's vital! In an essay, I can say almost anything I want, provided I can back up my argument with evidence. For example, I can argue that Germany won World War Two if I can provide evidence for that, maybe I would need to redefine the word 'won'.

However, you shouldn't make these obscure arguments just for the sake of making arguments – argue with the evidence, not against it. If you find that the evidence is pointing in a particular direction, maybe you should argue in that direction. A key to writing a successful essay is the evidence that you use – the stronger the evidence, the stronger your case, the stronger your essay.

## The Parts of an Essay

Before you can write a successful essay, you must understand the various parts of an essay. This is basic information but too many students try to get their essays written and out of the way without really understanding what the purpose of each part is and how to maximise their impact. Below we will briefly look at each part of an essay and what purposes they serve.

### Introduction

The introduction of an essay is the most important part. It comes first and provides the initial answers to the question. The introduction is important because it introduces the topic, your answers to the question and it sets the tone and quality for the rest of the essay. A reader should be able to assess your understanding of the topic and your answer to the question just by reading the introduction – everything else is just details. Too many students rush through the introduction and miss an opportunity to impress the reader.

## Body

As mentioned above, the body of the essay is where the details are discussed. This is where you provide your answers in depth, with evidence. An essay body is usually divided into paragraphs (or sections if it is large) and each paragraph deals with a new idea or argument. The body should discuss in depth what was covered briefly in the introduction. The body is where you expand your ideas, demonstrate your knowledge and argue your case. The body of your essay should confirm the assessment that the reader made after reading your introduction.

## Conclusion

The final part of the essay is the conclusion. Many people feel that conclusions are unnecessary, and from the perspective of the answer to the question, that could be true – conclusions add nothing new to the essay, but they do provide a smooth and clear finish to the arguments. Without a conclusion, an essay can feel as if it finished too abruptly, like the reader was left 'up in the air' and from a writing perspective it is always best to wrap up loose ideas and leave the reader with a sense of completion.

## The Hamburger Method

The Hamburger Method of essay writing is a process that I developed whilst teaching students how to write their best essays. It is a simple way to view the structure of an essay and it helps compartmentalise the planning while still maintaining coherence. The Hamburger Method can be summarised with the following diagram:

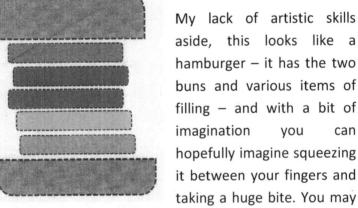

My lack of artistic skills aside, this looks like a hamburger – it has the two buns and various items of filling – and with a bit of imagination you can hopefully imagine squeezing it between your fingers and taking a huge bite. You may be wondering how this could possibly relate to writing an essay – bear with me.

Imagine that each of the elements of this hamburger are the parts of an essay: the buns are the introduction and the conclusion – they hold the essay together; each of the elements of filling are the paragraphs, or arguments, that make up the body of the essay. Just like a hamburger is better when eaten as a whole, so too is an essay better when it is read as a whole, but just like a hamburger can be taken apart, and each element eaten separately, so too should each part of the essay be understood when written separately.

When you look at an essay in this way – as a large item made up of smaller components – it becomes simpler to understand and easier to complete – it doesn't seem so overwhelming. Let's look at exactly how this hamburger concept translates into an effective essay and the process involved in turning your ideas into a coherent, clearly undertood and effective essay that will help to bring you the success you desire.

Examine the following diagram:

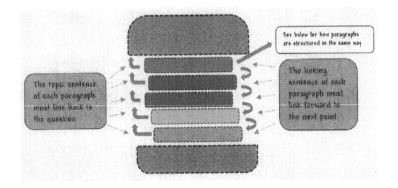

This is how the hamburger translates into your essay. Notice each of the components, which we will discuss in more detail below:

## The Introduction

The introduction is when you introduce your topic and add some context. It is also your first opportunity to answer the question. To be effective your introduction must do those two things. The answer should not be in detail – just some simple sentences listing your answers or arguments – you add detail and evidence later.

The introduction is the first part of the essay that the reader sees and it should make a good impression. If the reader feels good about the introduction they will generally feel good about the whole essay, but if the introduction leaves them feeling unsatisfied they will have that impression of the whole essay.

261

Your introduction should include some sentences introducing the topic and providing context for the question, then the questions should be rephrased in your own words, and finally your answers to the question provided simply and clearly.

## The Paragraphs

As shown in the diagram above, each paragraph is structured as a mini version of the hamburger. Rather than your paragraphs being held together by the 'buns' of introduction and conclusion the paragraph is held together by topic and linking sentences. The 'filling' of your burger is explanation and evidence, rather than individual paragraphs. This is demonstrated in the diagram below.

Each of your paragraphs should address one of your answers or arguments. I usually suggest five paragraphs (less is probably not enough to answer the question, and more can become tedious) but the exact number is up to you and the circumstances of the

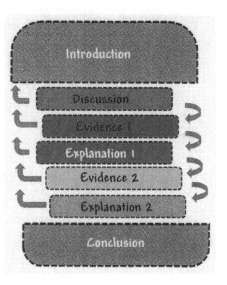

essay. As can be seen in the diagram above, the structure of a paragraph is like the structure of the whole essay – a hamburger, but the elements are different. Each paragraph begins with a topic sentence (or two) which introduces the idea or answer that will be the focus of the paragraph. This sentence must again rephrase the question in relation to the answer that you are discussing.

Next comes a couple of sentences which provide some discussion of the answer in more detail. This is followed by some evidence in support of your answer and then explanation of the relevance or significance of the evidence. It is usually a good idea to provide at least two different pieces of evidence, maybe more depending on the topic and expectations of the teacher. Remember, the more evidence you have the stronger your argument will be.

The final element of the paragraph is a sentence concluding the argument and linking it to the next paragraph. This link adds coherence to your essay and ensures that you do not get distracted from your purpose – which is to answer the question. If each paragraph utilises this structure you will find that the essay is easier to write and that your writing and ideas 'flow smoothly' from one to the next – this increases the sense of coherence that the reader feels when they read your essay.

## Topic Sentences

Topic sentences are an important part of your essay. They begin each paragraph and ensure that your ideas are coherent and logical. Ideally, a topic sentence does two things: it rephrases the question, and it provides one of your answers to the question. That answer will be the subject of the paragraph that begins with that topic sentence.

It is vital that each topic sentence does those two things – rephrase the question and provide an answer – because this not only keeps you on topic, but also lets your reader know that you are addressing the questions throughout your essay. Too many times I have read essays in which students have gone off-topic during their essay. They may still be discussing the topic but if they are not answering the question they are wasting time. Topic sentences serve to 'anchor' your writing to the question so that you stay on topic.

## Linking Sentences

Linking sentences are not necessary but they are recommended. Just like topic sentences link your paragraph back to the question, the linking sentences link each paragraph to the next one, thus creating a coherent unit. If you have planned your essay well each idea or argument should be similar or related. By linking them together you emphasise that relationship and strengthen your arguments.

Linking sentences also rephrase the question (again) and mention your answer (again). This emphasises your answer and ensures that the reader will not be able to miss it. By ending each of your paragraphs in this way you will create an essay that is easy to write and a structure in which your ideas are easy to follow

**The Conclusion**

The conclusion of an essay is your 'last word' on the topic – your last opportunity to reemphasise your ideas or arguments and answer the question. Nothing new should be brought up in your conclusion, instead you should briefly summarise your answers and state the significance of the answers or topic. A few sentences are enough to tie up any 'loose ends' in your essay and ensure that your writing is not open-ended.

# Essay Writing – an Example

Let's put everything we've just discussed into practise. We are going to write each of the components of the essay and then put them together so that you can see how it is done in practice. We'll work with a simple essay question that will be able to demonstrate the process.

Essay Question: *Sending kids to school is beneficial to society. Do you agree?*

1. Firstly, we must analyse the question – luckily this is a simple one. It's asking us to agree or disagree with a statement about sending kids to school. Remember, there is no right or wrong opinions, only good or bad arguments. As a part of this analysis we would define what 'beneficial' and 'society' means so that we can address the correct meanings.

2. Assume that we've done some brainstorming and have come up with lots of ideas which we have filtered – leaving us with a list of ideas.

3. We have decided to answer the question by agreeing that sending kids to school is beneficial to society because this is where the evidence leads us.

4. A simple essay plan listing our answer and reasons is as follows:

    a. I agree that sending kids to school is beneficial to society,

    b. Reason 1 – they learn knowledge – a smarter society,

c. Reason 2 – they learn skills – a more effective society,

d. Reason 3 – they learn discipline – a more ordered society,

e. Reason 4 – they learn co-operation – a friendlier society,

f. Reason 5 – it keeps them busy – a safer society,

This is a snapshot of our essay – our answer with five reasons – each reason will be a separate paragraph.

5. Now we need to write our introduction. Our introduction introduces the topic, adds context and provides our answers. We'll write one sentence for each point. It is basically Point 4 (above) in sentence form.

> *Sending children to school is compulsory in numerous countries because many people believe that school has multiple benefits to society. [introducing the topic] Benefits are advantages that are provided for society and there are several for attending school, and there are many benefits of school attendance. [defining key words]*

*These benefits include the acquisition of knowledge, the learning of new skills, the development of discipline, the learning of co-operation and that students are kept busy. [providing the answers]*

6. Now we need to write our paragraphs – one for each of our reasons. Each paragraph starts with a topic sentence which rephrases the question and provides the first answer. Like this:

   *The first benefit of sending kids to school [rephrasing the question] is the acquisition of knowledge. [your first answer]*

7. Next you need to discuss the answer in more detail. This can be with another sentence or two.

   *Knowledge is important because without it the population is ignorant and an ignorant population is one that cannot make effective decisions. By sending kids to school members of the society are ensuring that the future is more positive.*

8.  Next, we will provide some evidence to support our argument and explain how that evidence relates to the question. Evidence can be from a source, such as a book, or it can be an idea that supports your argument.

    *One example of this is during elections. When people have more knowledge, they can be more informed about political options and can therefore make better decisions. A better-informed electorate means that the politicians are more accountable and will be forced to perform better.*

9.  Now we add another piece of evidence to support the argument.

    *Another example of the benefit of knowledge to society is with the training of the workforce. The more knowledge people have the better able to enter the workforce they will be. This will affect the economy in positive ways such as increased employment and reduced workplace injuries.*

10. Finally, our linking sentence says something about the significance of this idea and connects it with the next one.

   *Knowledge that is gained at school is of vital benefit to society and helps it to operate smoothly but also of importance are the skills that people develop.*

11. Now let's put each of these elements together to form our first paragraph.

   *The first benefit of sending kids to school is the acquisition of knowledge. Knowledge is important because without it the population is ignorant and an ignorant population is one that cannot make effective decisions. By sending kids to school members of the society are ensuring that the future is more positive. One*

270

*example of this is during elections. When people have more knowledge, they can be more informed about political options and can therefore make better decisions. A better-informed electorate means that politicians are more accountable and will be forced to perform better. Another example of the benefit of knowledge to society is with the training of the workforce. The more knowledge people have the better able to enter the workforce they will be. This will affect the economy in positive ways such as increased employment and reduced workplace injuries. Knowledge that is gained at school is a vital benefit to society and helps it to operate smoothly but also of importance are the skills that people develop.*

12. Now we continue this process for each of the paragraphs in our essay – the same structure for each paragraph – only the ideas will change.

13. Finally, we are ready to write our conclusion. The conclusion is a brief rephrasing of the question, a summary of your answers and a final statement of significance to wrap up.

> *The benefits of school are unmistakable. Knowledge, skills, discipline, co-operation and being kept busy all provide young people with greater chances of success for the future. This clearly demonstrates that schools must be supported for the good of society.*

This very simple example has been provided to show you the process of writing an essay. It may seem complicated but it doesn't have to be – if the essay is broken down into its basic components and each component is structured according to the 'Hamburger Method' it will be quicker and easier to write, and the end product will be much better. Try it and see how much difference some basic planning and organisation can make.

## Writing Essays Action Plan

1. Practise simple essay planning by creating sample essay questions and planning the essay

that you could write. These plans don't need to be complicated, and they can be about anything. For example, "Apples are better than bananas" is a question, a simple essay plan could be:

> Apples are better than bananas because:
> 1. They don't need to be peeled,
> 2. They don't get squashed in your bag,
> 3. They are juicier,

Repeating this process with multiple made-up essay questions (for best effect they should be about topics that you are studying) will improve your speed and skill at planning essays.

# Part 11 – Exams

*Keep the flame of curiosity and wonderment alive, even when studying for boring exams.*

Michio Kaku

Unfortunately, exams are a necessary evil. Although there are many issues with examining students via exams they are one of the easiest ways to test knowledge, and until someone can develop a better way they are here to stay. That is why it is vital to understand how to be successful in exams.

When exams are mentioned to most students they are usually overcome with feelings of dread and desperation. They picture rows of desks, the clock ticking loudly, the stern exam supervisors, and their own palms become sweaty – but it doesn't have to be that way. Exams are not mysterious or magical and simple planning and preparation can prepare anyone to be successful in a sit-down exam. Let's look at some of the ways that you can be successful in your exams.

# Preparation

The most important part of exam success (just like in anything else) is preparation. If you prepare adequately you can achieve almost anything. Preparation takes forethought, that is, you cannot start preparing one day before the event, you must think it through in advance to give yourself time to make the necessary plans and take the necessary steps.

**Short Term to Long Term Preparation**

Preparation falls into two categories: short term and long term preparation. Both types of preparation require a level of planning and organisation (see Part 6 – Planning and Organisation) which will enable you to divide up your study into easily manageable pieces.

Your long-term preparation involves you knowing when your exams occur months in advance. Most schools will have these dates arranged the year before, especially with external government exams. If not, you may still be able to determine approximately the weeks in which the exams occur and that should give you an idea of the time frames with which you are working.

Once you know when the exams occur you can begin to plan your study regime. Mark the exams on your calendar and work out how many weeks you have until they start (remember, this may include holidays). Now you can begin your short-term planning.

Short term plans involve working out what you will be studying each week and each day. You should have some idea about the topics that will be examined in the exam – if you don't then you need to find that information. Work out how many topics there are and how they fit into the time remaining until the exams start. For example, if there are 11 different topics to be covered in a Science exam and there are 18 weeks until the exam then you have one week to study each topic with seven weeks to revise everything again and fix any gaps in your understanding.

Now that you have prepared an overview of your study you can focus on the day-to-day elements of studying – we'll look at these soon. It's important to remember that successful exam study takes a long time, that's why you need to plan. There may be some people that tell you they can walk into an exam without studying and achieve great results. That may be true – they are either geniuses or very lucky, but they will not be able to rely on whatever it is for too much longer – eventually their genius is going to fade or their luck will run out. Either way it doesn't help you – that's why you need to prepare and study.

# Attitude

One of the reasons why this book started by discussing attitude is that an appropriate frame of mind is vital to success. Exams are no different – if you have the right attitude as you prepare for and sit exams your chances of being successful are much greater. Let's look at what the 'right' attitude means.

### Be Positive

Firstly, you must have a positive attitude if you want to be successful in your exams. We spent a bit of time talking about the power of a positive attitude at the start of the book so we won't repeat it here, except to emphasise its importance. To be successful a positive attitude must always be linked with effective study. Examine the following and consider its implications:

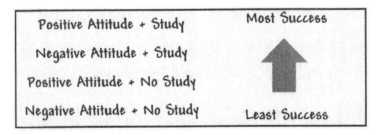

As demonstrated above, even if you do no study but you have a positive attitude you will do better than if you had a negative attitude without study. Similarly, if you study but have a negative attitude you will not do as well as if you study but have a positive attitude. In this regard exams are like exercise – you can go further and do better if you think you can <u>and</u> you put the training in.

**Don't Panic**

Secondly, and closely linked with a positive attitude, is the requirement to stay calm and not panic. This may be easier said than done, but if you have done the work and you have a positive attitude then panic has no place in your life. Panic is simply the loss of control and the overwhelming feeling of hopelessness. If you have done the preparation for the exam then you are still in control, and if you are confident that you will do well then there is no reason to feel hopeless.

If you feel the panic beginning to surface as exams approach (or on the day) then simply verbalise your positive attitude and convince yourself that you are in control, you've done the work and this exam is going to be no problem to you. If you have utilised the following strategies then this shouldn't be too difficult.

# Strategies

There are many strategies that you can adopt to improve your chances in exams. These all essentially do the same thing – improve your ability to understand and remember information which can be used in the exam. There are many others but these are some of the most common and effective.

**Flash Cards**

Flash cards are just like picture cards used to teach small children numbers and letters, except that they have facts or information related to the topic you are studying. To create effective flash cards, you need to identify key facts, or information on your topic – something that can be summarised in a few key words or phrases. For example, if my topic was the history of the Enlightenment in Europe I may include key individuals like Rousseau, Voltaire and Kant, with pictures, key dates and descriptions. Flash cards must be brief – something that can be glanced at to view important information. Flash cards can be colour-coded, numbered or marked in other ways to organise and identify them.

To use flash cards once they have been prepared simply take a set with you (a 'set' could be a topic, a section or a subject, depending on how much you wish to study) and when you have a moment spare (such as on a bus or in an elevator) pull them out and memorise them with quick glances. You may also add questions to the reverse of each card to test yourself.

- *ACTION – rather than waiting until you need to use them, create a stack of blank flashcards now. You may choose to buy them or make them yourself, just prepare them so that when you are ready to begin you have a pile waiting on your desk.*

### Diagrams

It is said that a picture is worth a thousand words, and it's very true. That's why diagrams are an effective way to help you organise and remember ideas. They do not need to be artistic, quality productions, or even anything meaningful – simply a graphic representation of an idea. Diagrams are good because they are simple to create and easy to remember, but they can represent very complex ideas. A well-known example of this is the 'tree of life' in biology. This represents the supposed development of life on prehistoric Earth and although it is not scientifically exact it demonstrates complex ideas that would take pages to explain in words.

In the same way, you can use simple diagrams to represent your ideas or concepts. The causes of the American Civil War can be represented by a flower – a petal for each cause. The subject of the diagram doesn't need to be related to the topic to be effective, or it can be directly related to the topic – to remember the bones in the human hand a diagram of the hand made up of bone-names could be used. Lists of facts can be turned into ladders, trains, rivers or shapes. There is no limit to how you can represent your ideas and you will find that remembering diagrams is easier than trying to remember words, because after all, we think in pictures, not words.

## Mind Maps

Mind maps are like diagrams when it comes to remembering information, but they are a little different because mind maps show more of the relationships between factors, ideas or individuals and they don't necessarily translate well into pictures or patterns. A mind map is simply a network or 'web' of factors which all link to a central idea. Mind maps can be as simple or as complex as you desire and they are a great way to explore and idea or the relationships between things.

## Summaries

Summaries are a good study method because they enable you to squeeze a lot of information into a relatively small space. Put simply, a summary involves taking out the extra 'stuff' in a paragraph or chapter or section and having only the most important facts and information remain. The process of writing the summary is probably the most valuable part of summaries – this forces you to think about what is and what is not important in a piece of writing and focus only on the important 'bits'.

You can use summaries to gain a better understanding of paragraphs, chapters or even whole books. Once the summary has been completed it can be easily reread and rewritten to aid memory and doesn't require a lot of reading to gain the desired information.

**Rewriting**

Another valuable strategy in exam preparation is rewriting. By rewriting I mean writing out passages by hand. These passages can be from books, websites (just be aware of potential plagiarism issues) or your own notes. The value of rewriting for exam preparation is that it forces you to think about the words and ideas you are copying, and the very process of writing increases the chances of you remembering what you are writing. What you rewrite does not need to be kept, and it can be done many times for the same passage – the more times you rewrite the more you will remember.

# Analyse the Exam

To be successful in an exam it is vital that you understand the exam and all its elements. This includes its structure, format, expectations, and types of questions. If you have an awareness of these elements you will be able to better prepare for the exam and will be more comfortable sitting it.

So how do you learn about these elements? The best way is to study past exams. Most exams use a similar structure and format each year (obviously, the questions change) and it is often possible to find past exam copies on government education websites. There are even companies which specialise in producing practise exams in the correct format.

You may also be able to gain some information about your exam by asking your teacher. They won't give you the exact questions but they can still provide you with some very useful information.

When you have a copy of a past exam spend some time analysing it.

- Look at the types of questions — (don't worry about what the exact questions are because they will change) are they multiple choice, short answer, paragraph answer, or essay questions?

- How many sections is the exam divided into? Are they the same size?
- What are the instructions for the exam? What are the items that are/are not permitted into the exam?
- What are each of the questions worth? Are some sections worth more than others?

Asking questions like these will give you a better understanding of what to expect in your exam. This will assist you with your study – you can focus on those parts of the exam that are worth more. It will also help you deal with the potential stress of an exam – if you know what's coming you have less to fear. Either way, learning as much about your upcoming exam will help you succeed with it.

**Time Planning**

Another important part of analysing the exam is working out its time parameters. This means you will calculate the approximate time you can spend on each section and question. This is determined by the value and difficulty of each question. For example, you should not spend too much time on a question that is only worth a few marks at the expense of a question that is worth many. This is something that should be worked out before the exam is attempted. Let's look at an example:

You have an exam which is 90 minutes in length.
It is composed of three sections
    A. Multiple Choice worth 20 marks
    B. Short Answer worth 20 marks
    C. Essay worth 60 marks

One simple way of dividing up your time is as follows:
    Planning time: 10 minutes (I use a rough
estimate of 10% for planning time)
    Section A: 15 minutes
    Section B: 15 minutes
    Section C: 45 Minutes
    Review time: 5 minutes
    Total: 90 minutes
As you can see the time allocated for Section C is three times as much as the other two sections because it is worth three times as much.

If this planning cannot be done before the exam it must be done during the planning time and once these times have been decided you must keep to them. Don't make the mistake of ignoring or forgetting the time restraints you have set. If you get carried away on the questions on Section B that leaves you less time for Section C and that is the most valuable one.

# Practise Exams

One of the best ways that you can prepare for exams is by doing them – practise exams, that is. Nothing can prepare you for the pressure and tension of an exam as well as an exam that provides you with some pressure and tension – even if it is just pretend. Practise exams have been used for a long time to prepare students for the 'real thing', and these days there are numerous sources of them. Government education websites, companies that specialise in practise exams and even your teacher may be able to provide you with some.

The best way to utilise practise exams is to set the same time parameters as the real exam – if the real one is two hours then your practise should be two hours. Try to emulate the same conditions as the real exam – if you will be doing the real exam on a small desk, don't do the practise while you are sitting on a sofa. Also use the same materials you are permitted to take with you into the real exam room.

You can choose to conduct practise exams as open- or closed-book exams. An open-book exam means that you have the textbook or books open next to you when you sit the practise exam – when you need to find an answer you search the books and then write it down. This type of test should only be done initially, when you are not confident about the exam. It will help you learn some of the information but it will not really prepare you for the 'exam experience'.

A closed-book practise exam is the more traditional way of doing it – you have only the exam and your brain. This can be more stressful but it gives you a better idea of the real thing and it also gives you a clear indication of what areas need to be improved. If you are able (and they are willing) ask your teacher to check your exam (use the word 'check', not 'mark') and provide some feedback about how you went.

This process can provide you with an accurate idea of how you will perform on the real exam, but like with anything the more practise you do the more you will improve. I recommend one practise exam per week in the months leading up to the real exam – it will take time but it will be worthwhile. You don't even need to do the entire exam in one sitting – divide it up and complete one section each night. If you are keeping to the time limits it will still benefit you.

## On the Day

If you have done all the preparation that you can you should be quite confident on the day of the exam. Now that you have reached the end of that long road of study and stress it is important to relax and remember that there is nothing else that you can do to prepare – if it's not done by now it's too late! But there are things that you can still do to maximise your chances and ensure that the actual exam experience will be smooth. Make the following things a part of your 'exam day routine'.

## Breakfast

We've all heard that breakfast is the most important meal of the day, and I've already emphasised the importance of that meal in this book. I won't repeat the same information except to say that breakfast is doubly important on the morning of an exam. For an exam, you need to be at your peak – not just during the one, two or three hours when you are writing, but in the hours before the exam when your natural tension means that you will be burning through energy faster than normal. Without breakfast (or with an unhealthy one) your energy reserves will quickly be depleted and you will find yourself tired and lacking motivation. In most cases that will usually be right in the middle of the exam when you need it most.

## Spare Tools

There's nothing worse than having lots to say, knowing that it's right, but being unable to write it down. That's what may happen in your exam if your pen stops working and you don't have any spares. That is why it is important to ensure that you have plenty of spare equipment before you enter the exam room. Depending on the exam you may need pens, pencils, rulers and erasers. Any of these items could be vital to complete the exam successfully so if your pen runs out of ink or your pencil breaks having a spare could save you.

It is a good idea to prepare a simple equipment bag, in which you keep extra pens, pencils, etc., well before your first exam. Take it to each of your exams if you are permitted and replace items as they are used. If there are problems you can relax knowing that you have spares, if there are no problems you haven't lost anything and you have a few extra pencils to use. You will regret not having one if you need it.

### Watch the Clock

'Watching the clock' means keeping track of the time and it is vital for exam success. If you have analysed and planned your exam you will have an idea of what the time parameters of the exam are – you will know how long you can spend on each section and each question. This planning and keeping to the allotted time is very important – if you have organised your time according to what is most valuable in the exam you will be focusing on those elements that can benefit you the most. If you keep to the arranged times you will not be focusing your time on the less valuable parts of the exam.

To 'watch the clock' effectively you should have a wrist watch which you place on the desk in front of you – it should be easy to see so that you can know how much time is left on a particular question. An inexpensive watch will be fine for this purpose as it only needs to be used during these exam times. Avoid smart watches or other 'smart' devices as they will probably not be permitted into the exam room. If you are unable to have a watch then you will need to watch the clock that is provided in the room. This is usually a wall clock or clock projected onto a screen. Either way, ensure that you can keep track of the time, and when the time you set for a question has been reached stop and move onto the next question – even if you have not finished it. You may have time left over at the end of the exam to finish these questions but it is better to have some unfinished questions than questions which have not even been attempted at all.

### Review the Exam

Reviewing the exam is a simple but useful process that can take place before you write anything. With most exams, there is a period of five to 15 minutes which is designated as 'reading time'. During this time, you are not permitted to write anything but can only read through the exam. Most students don't understand the value of reading time and after quickly glancing through the exam will spend the rest of the time staring off into space waiting for the 'actual' exam to begin. Don't make this mistake! Reading time is an opportunity to evaluate the questions in the exam and determine which ones you should be spending your time on when 'writing time' begins.

Read each question and answer it in your mind – do you know the answer? Are you able to begin formulating your response? Do you need to think about it? Do you need to remember some particular facts, formulae or information? The very process of asking these questions and thinking about your responses will prompt your subconscious mind to begin coming up with answers. Even as you move onto other questions your mind will be processing responses to the questions you have already passed and when you come back to it during writing time your response will be quicker and more complete. That's 15 minutes that is better used than staring at the wall!

## Read the Question

Valuable advice about exams that I have given to students for many years is to 'read the question'. This may seem too obvious to worry about but it is amazing how many students fail to do it adequately. Reading the question means spending some time considering exactly what the question is asking, not what you think it's asking, or what it seems to be asking. Let me explain: Some questions are straight forward, but many are not. Many questions, especially at the senior end of high school, have multiple elements, subtle or hidden implications and phrases or clauses added to mislead the unwary.

One mistake many students make is to read only the first part of a question with multiple parts – you're tired, you've been sitting down for over an hour, you're running out of time and you see the following question:

> List the five countries where the greatest levels of deforestation take place, and explain the impacts that it is having on those countries.

Many students, in the rush to get the exam finished, see the first part of the question, list the five countries and then move on to the next question. What they don't realise is that the second part of the question is a 'higher order' question – meaning it takes more thinking to answer – and thus will be the more important part of the question. A complete answer requires the 'listing' and the 'explaining' in that question. A quick analysis will ensure you do not miss that.

Another element of questions that students often miss are the hidden or subtle implications in questions. Look at the following example:

> Using your own and extended knowledge describe the causes of the Russian Revolution of 1917.

Most students will focus on 'describe the causes of' and write what they learned in class, but they will fail to see the implications of 'using your own and extended knowledge' – this means that your teacher is expecting you to add information that was not covered in class, either from extra reading that was provided to you or extra reading that you undertook yourself. Failing to recognise this will rob you of the extra marks you could get for this question.

A final way that student exam results can be reduced is by misreading additions to questions. A single word can change the meaning of a question and trap many students. Consider the following example:

> Which of the following are not nouns?

Many students will see 'following' and 'nouns' but fail to see 'not'. Obviously, they will not provide the correct answer – not because they don't know it but because they did not read the question. These simple examples demonstrate the importance of reading the question carefully before answering it, and not rushing into the wrong answer.

**Plan**

As I've said many times before – planning is probably the most important part of any enterprise. Without planning any task becomes unclear and the finished result uncertain. It is just the same with exams. For an exam to be completed successfully it requires planning on two levels: the entire exam must be planned, and each section must be planned. Let's look at how this will work.

Firstly, the *entire* exam must be planned. This process starts during reading time and should be the first task that is completed when writing time begins. As discussed in 'Analyse the Exam' the process of planning the timing of the exam involves calculating how much time each section should take you to complete. This is dependent upon how much each section is worth and the total time of the exam. If done effectively it should enable you to concentrate on those parts of the exam which will give you the most benefit.

Secondly, each *section* of the exam needs to be planned before starting it. Of course, this depends upon what type of questions the section contains. For example, sections containing multiple choice or short answer questions do not need to be planned – you just start at the top and work your way down – but larger, more complex questions, like paragraph and essay questions, must be planned before they can be effectively completed. This planning may seem like a waste of time but it is necessary for effective writing. Very few people can write effectively without planning something first – if you are one of those people then you probably don't need to be reading this book – for everyone else planning is a necessity.

As I've said before, I use the formula of approximately 10% of the task time for planning – so if you have calculated the required time of an exam section at 30 minutes then 3 minutes of that time should be taken up by planning. The longer and more important the section is the more time you should spend planning it. So how do you plan your answer?

The planning process is basically determining the structure of your answer. You should consider the following questions:

- What are your main points or arguments? Writing them in a list is helpful.
- What is your most important point or argument? This should go first.
- How much space do you have to answer the question? Do you have limited or unlimited space? If it is limited you should plan to use all of it.
- In what ways can you 'extend' your answer if desired?

Once you have considered these questions create a quick plan of your answer. This can be done either in the space provided, on a blank part of the exam or on blank paper – many teachers like to see your plans, they provide insight into your thinking and can make the marking easier – check with your teacher on this point.

Let's look at a simple example: You have a question asking you to briefly explain why the North won the American Civil War. You remember four basic reasons: the North had a stronger economy, a larger population, a more powerful navy and the slaves were a disadvantage to the South. Your quick plan looks like this:

Introduction
Part 1 – North stronger economy
Part 2 – North larger population
Part 3 – North more powerful navy
Part 4 – South slaves disadvantage
Conclusion

Depending on the space you are allowed, each of these parts could be a sentence or a paragraph, but now you have an idea about what you are writing and your answer is going to be clear and well structured. This process can be used on a small or a large question, it does not take long but without it your answer will not be as effective as it would be with it.

### Do What you Know First

A simple but important principle of exams is to do what you know first. Now, I am expecting that because you are reading this book and will have done adequate preparation for the exam you will know everything in the exam. But if you haven't done the preparation, or there are elements of the exam that you still do not know, it is vital that you do those parts of the exam that you know before the other parts.

Why? Your purpose in the exam is to maximise the number of marks that you receive and you get marks by demonstrating your knowledge of material learned in class. If you spend time trying to come up with information when you are not totally sure of it you risk not having enough time to answer the questions that you do know – and hence miss chances for a better result.

So, during reading time note any questions that you do not know the answers to, or seem too difficult, and keep them for last – then you can concentrate on getting top marks for the information that you know.

### Leave Nothing Blank

Another important principle is to leave nothing blank on your exam paper. One of the worst mistakes a student can make in an exam is to leave questions unanswered – this guarantees they will receive no marks for that question! As discussed above, there may be questions that you do not know the answer to, or find it difficult to remember the answer. Even if you don't know the answer it is important that you write something down anyway, rather than nothing. Try to come up with something that is relevant to the topic – you should have a vague idea from your notes, reading or memory. Plan it out just like you would a regular question, and write your answer. If your answer is not totally accurate you may be close to an answer, and even if you are not your teacher may award you with some marks just for trying – some marks are better than none!

## Use Every Second

Finally, ensure that you use every second of your exam time. I've lost count of the number of times I've seen students sitting around for the last 30 minutes of their exam doing nothing. When I approach, this is how the interaction usually goes:

> "Why aren't you writing?"
> "I've finished."
> "Okay, then why don't you check it?"
> "I did."
> "Then check it again."
> "Why?"

They usually roll their eyes and pretend to check their exam until I walk away. This is a typical response. These students don't see the need to maximise their results – they don't have the drive for success – they just want the exam to finish so that they can go onto something more fun. As someone who wants to be successful and knows that future success requires present sacrifice you won't be like those students.

If you do finish the exam earlier (and the only valid reason for that is that the exam was easier than you thought and you finished it sooner than you planned) then the rest of the time should be spent on reviewing and improving your answers. Upon a second reading, many answers can be expressed in a more fluent way, can be made clearer, or extra points and explanation added. This review could mean a few extra marks which would have been lost if you had simply sat and waited for the time to pass.

## Exams Action Plan

1. Check your calendar right now and determine when your exams are scheduled. How many weeks do you have to prepare?
2. Explore sources of practise exams that you can use for your study.
3. Prepare an 'exam kit' which contains spare equipment.

# Part 12 – Technology

*Every aspect of human technology has a dark side, including the bow and arrow.*

*Margaret Atwood*

Technology is a part of our lives and is becoming more so every year – so much so that those of you who are in school are called "digital natives" – meaning that you have grown up with technology and don't know life without it. Technology can be very helpful, enabling us to do more things more quickly, but it can also get in the way. It is very important to use technology in way that will advantage you, not hinder you, and not simply use it because it is there. Following are some ways to use (or not use) technology to your advantage.

## The Internet

The Internet is nothing special to young people these days, but I can clearly remember when there was no Internet, or email, or social networking. When you wanted to contact someone, you used a telephone, or wrote a letter. A lot has changed! In fact, so much has changed that many people cannot live without being 'online'. Now, people expect to be in contact with their friends any time, all the time.

In relation to being successful at high school this constant connection certainly has its advantages: it's easy and convenient to contact friends, or teachers, for help; researching an endless supply of sources is easy; storing and accessing documents is safe and convenient; and technology can be used almost anywhere. But there are disadvantages, too: the constant contact makes it difficult to 'disconnect' and relax; there is the ever-present threat of predators; technology regularly breaks down; and it's difficult to know what can be trusted online.

Just like any technology tool you must use the Internet with a clear understanding of the benefits and risks, and not get caught in the trap of 'tech addiction'. Use it when it is helpful and don't use it when it is not – be purposeful with your Internet access and don't just use it because it is there. If you do use it for research ensure that your information is verified with more than one source and never share personal information over the Internet.

## Writing vs Typing

These days typing is becoming the normal way to record information – we type our ideas or notes on our phones, laptops, tablets and desktop computers. It's quick, easy and convenient for storing work for later – but is it the best way? Most people don't write things down on paper with a pen any more – but have we lost something by embracing the 'new' technology?

Numerous studies have shown that using a pen and paper to record ideas and notes, and for writing generally, increases understanding and memorisation. There's something about the process of physically writing with your hand that increases the effectiveness of the brain. There is a connection between nerves of the hand and the brain which means that use of the hand to write notes strengthens certain neurons in the brain. It's something that can be used to increase your own effectiveness.

So, does that mean that you should throw away your computer, and mobile phone? Not necessarily! Writing by hand works best with your brain but there are still many advantages to using technology for writing. It can be quicker and easier, it's easier to organise and store efficiently, and it is more secure – I'm writing this book digitally (using my desktop PC and my Surface) because I can access it anywhere, store it in the cloud and never worry about losing it. Things that I've written on paper have been less simple. However, I still use paper and a pen when I am thinking, planning and need to 'work through' a sentence or paragraph. The point is, use a combination of both technology and conventional writing, depending on the circumstances and what serves you best.

## Podcasts and Audiobooks

Podcasts are a relatively new phenomenon – the development of mobile technology has made them easier to access and fuelled a growth in their popularity. Now you can find a podcast on almost any topic. Some of them are for entertainment but many of them are for growth and personal development. You can find a podcast to help you develop in areas such as relationships, time management, goals, and the list goes on. Podcasts range in length from a few minutes to a few hours and can be professionally produced or made in someone's garage. It is also possible to produce your own podcasts using the right software. You can produce your own 'study podcasts' which you can save for yourself or share with friends. They will enable you to study anytime.

Audiobooks have a similar history and range – an audiobook is a digital production of a published book – they can be of best-selling novels or classic works of literature, produced and marketed on professional websites (such as Audible.com) or produced by volunteers and available free on community websites (such as Librevox.com). I use these and other sites and have a large audio library.

Podcasts and audiobooks are great because they are so portable – you can listen to them anywhere, at any time, but they are most useful at the times when you would not normally be reading (walking, exercising, riding, etc.). These enable you 'read' and learn more than you normally would. Just by 'reading' audiobooks books while I am walking or driving I can read an extra one or two books each month. In addition to their portability audiobooks also aid memorisation, as hearing things can help you remember things that just reading them will not.

- *ACTION – check to see if you have a podcast app on your phone (I'm assuming you already have a phone), if not, get one. Spend a bit of time searching and subscribe to a few podcasts which interest you and will help you be successful. Now, when you head out you can use your travel time more effectively.*

## Audio Notes

Like podcasts, audio notes have many benefits: they are portable, sharable, easy to produce and store, and aid memorisation. So, what are audio notes? They are simply notes that you have created and recorded in an audio format. Audio notes can be produced in a professional way using the correct software or they can be recorded quickly using your mobile phone. Either way they are a great way to keep track of ideas and thoughts that can be reviewed repeatedly

## Controlling Screens

Earlier in the book we touched on the problems with computer screens – they can have a negative impact on your eyes and your brain, and modify your lifestyle in a way that will not be best for you. Plenty of research has been done on these impacts so we won't go into the details here but they all agree that the overwhelming use of screens in our modern world needs to be seriously considered.

Despite knowing this, it's difficult to reduce the screens in our lives, but you must be able to do that if you wish to be successful. At least being able to 'control' the screens in your life is vital. By 'control' I mean NOT being on a screen most hours of each day without even realising it. Think about a typical day for a student at your school: They are woken up by their phone, use their phone to play music while they are getting ready, read social media posts on the way to school, communicate with friends and keep up with the latest trends during the school day (even if phones are not permitted at school), much of the work at school is done on tablets or laptop computers, more social media on the way home, then messaging with friends, playing games, watching TV or streaming video until late when the phone comes out again and pings notifications all night. This day has very little purposeful non-screen time.

Currently, little time is set aside for doing things without screens, such as reading and quiet time. We've talked about the importance of both these activities but screens get in the way of quality reading and quiet time, and there are other activities such as sleeping and family time that would be better without the constant interruptions. We've also just looked at the value of writing over typing. The point is that you should be making the conscious decision to use technology, or NOT use technology, based upon the advantages or disadvantages for that activity. When you can do that you will be able to maximise the effectiveness of the activity and your involvement in it.

## Videos

Most of you will not remember video tapes – the large plastic boxes holding digital tape that were inserted into video players to play movies or other programs. Back when I was in school they were the latest thing and were enthusiastically used to show all manner of educational programs. These days the same thing is done in less time with a better result using DVDs, Blu-ray, USB, streaming and online. There is now very little that cannot be found in some video form.

This is significant because the potential for a wide range of topics is endless and the possibility of finding instructional videos that can be helpful is great. You've probably already encountered this on YouTube: do you need to know how to fix a leaky tap? Or how to clock the latest console game? Or how to hack a laptop? Find a video that shows you, step by step, how to do it. This works just as well for school-related topics. Do you need to know how to write a killer science report? Or how to throw a perfect curve ball? Or construct an unbeatable argument? Find a video.

Videos are helpful because, not only can they be found on a wide variety of topics, but they are produced by a wide variety of people – that can be helpful because everyone teaches in a different way. One video might be difficult to understand but a video about the very same topic produced by someone else could be just what you were looking for. The style of teaching may be different from your regular teacher and the different perspective may help you understand better.

So, use videos to improve your understanding when you are having trouble grasping an idea or concept, or simply use them to gain a wider and deeper understanding of a topic with which you are already familiar. Either way videos can assist you to become more successful – you can even think about creating your own to share with others.

## Note-Taking Apps

Earlier we spent some time talking about the importance of taking notes effectively, and how to do that. Now, I'd like to talk about how you can do that digitally. We've already looked at some of the benefits of electronic methods of study and note-taking apps are one of the ways you can take advantage of that. Note-taking apps make it easier to take, organise, store and share notes.

There are lots of note-taking apps out there (probably hundreds) but I've found that the best ones are OneNote and Evernote. OneNote was a part of Microsoft's Office suite but can now be used on its own and Evernote is a standalone app that was probably one of the first successful note-taking apps. Both apps have free and paid versions and can be used on almost any device, both are easy to learn but take a little bit of time to master, and both have about the same functionality.

With a good note-taking app (like the two mentioned above) you can take type- or hand-written notes (if your device recognises stylus input); add input such as diagrams, graphics, hyperlinks, video and audio files, screen captures and many other useful actions. You can also organise your notes into notebooks, pages and subpages, print your notes and share them via email or the cloud.

I have used OneNote for years and find it a very valuable tool. I have it divided into work and personal notebooks and access it on my tablet at work, my desktop at home and on my phone when I'm out and about. It saves automatically so I know that whatever I write is going to be backed-up to my OneDrive account and will be ready on whatever device I choose to use next. I particularly like that my wife can add an item to our shared shopping list which will automatically update whilst I am out doing the shopping.

Of course, the note-taking app that you use will be based mainly on personal preference – although they all do basically the same things there are differences. Some do one thing better than the others, some are a bit easier to familiarise yourself with, and some just look better. Use whatever works for you. So, try some, see how they make your life (and study) easier and choose the one that 'clicks' with the way you do things.

## The Cloud

'The Cloud' is something that has developed relatively recently but for you 'digital natives' it's as familiar as, well, clouds! If you are not familiar with the Cloud it is basically an online storage and access platform for all your digital content – documents, music, pics, video and any other files. I'm mentioning it here because, just like note-taking apps, the Cloud can make study easier and more convenient.

Imagine that your work is sucked up into the clouds when you finish with it and it's ready to be accessed from anywhere when you want. This service provides a level of security and convenience that was unknown up until the present. The Cloud enables you to keep your files safe for your own access but also to share them like never before. The possibilities for collaboration with the Cloud are almost endless. You can have a group of people, around the world all working on the same document in real time and communicating with each other via voice or video while they do it, if that is possible then working collaboratively with your study group looks easy.

Just like with note-taking apps there are many Cloud services to choose from and most of them, but not all, are free, or have free options. All the big tech companies have these Cloud services including Microsoft with OneDrive, Google with Google Drive and Apple with iCloud, and there are many quality services from smaller companies such as DropBox and Box. Just like with note-taking apps try them all and use whichever one serves your purposes best.

## Gaming

You may ask what a section on gaming is doing in a book about success at high school. Well, the truth is that gaming is a part of life and it would be unrealistic of me to say, "if you want to succeed at high school there should be no gaming!" – that may be accurate but for those of you who are into gaming it is possible to continue your passion AND succeed at high school. The catch is, of course, that you will not be able to play games as much as you would like: no more late-night gaming sprees, 8-hour game sessions, or face-stuck-to-a-screen-where-ever-you-are sessions. As I've said before, to succeed at high school you will need 'balance' and that means you will need to prioritise games lower down your list of importance.

Building short game sessions into your personal timetable can help you control how much time you 'waste' on gaming. In fact, using these game sessions as a reward for completing work or assignments is a good motivational tool, especially when you tie it in with the work of others — for example, arrange to meet online with friends after everyone has completed their homework.

Something to be wary of with gaming is if it becomes your substitute for exercise. Believe it or not, but running a marathon in a computer game has little physical benefit for you, and may even be hazardous to your health – remember Pokémon Go? You must ensure that your breaks from study are not filled with gaming – do something physical rather than another activity involving sitting down. A possibility may be the use of gaming sensors like the Xbox Kinect. With the correct games, you can turn a study break-gaming session into a healthy workout – it's better than nothing, but not as good as a run in the fresh air.

So, don't stop gaming: reduce it, plan it and use it to benefit you and motivate you to achieve the best you can in your studies. You will find that the less gaming you take part in the more you will enjoy and appreciate it, and the more grateful you will be at the end of high school when you achieve your great results.

## Technology Action Plan

1. Create technology-free 'zones' within your personal timetable – periods of time in which you turn off your devices. Use this time to think, reflect and relax.
2. Install a podcast app on your devices (if you don't already have one) and explore podcasts that will help you to succeed at high school. Choose some times when you can listen to these podcasts on a regular basis – while you are exercising is a good option.
3. Install one or all the main note-taking apps on your devices (if you don't already have one) and experiment with them for a few weeks. Choose the one which works for you and begin making it a part of your planning and organisation.

# Part 13 – Myths

This section of the book will address some very powerful myths that are believed around the world. A myth – a widely believed idea that is not true – has power because it can change a person's thoughts and behaviour. People have a way of making myths true by believing in them and acting as if they were true, but it doesn't have to be that way. If you defy a myth – that is, refuse to believe in it – you take away its power. Let's look at some of the most common myths related to succeeding in high school and take away their power.

### I'm Not 'Smart' Enough

I've heard the expression "I'm (or He's or She's) not smart enough" too many times in the past. It has come from students, parents and even (unfortunately) teachers. The idea behind this myth is that a student is not capable of doing well in a particular subject – or even high school generally – because they are just not smart enough. Their mental capacity has reached a ceiling and they are unable to rise above it. This can be one of the most powerful and most damaging of myths. By calling this a myth I am not saying that some people are smart and others are not, but what I am saying is that you don't need to be smart to succeed at high school.

As you hopefully learned by reading this book the keys to success at high school are the right mindset, organisation and hard work – you don't need to be 'smart' to make use of these things. In fact, I've known 'smart' students who haven't succeeded and students who weren't considered smart who have because they had the right mindset, were organised and worked hard. It can be a difficult pattern to break but don't give this myth any power.

### Multitasking

The myth of multitasking has been around for years. Strangely enough, I've heard it most often from students who have been trying to convince me that they can listen to music and write at the same time. These students may think (and hope) that they can work effectively whilst focusing on more than one thing but the evidence says otherwise. Numerous studies have shown that when it comes to completing tasks there is no such thing as multitasking – what takes place when a person tries to focus on more than one thing can be described either as 'rapid shuffling' or 'brain division'.

The bottom line is that any time you try to do more than one thing at the same time each of the things you are trying to do is only getting a portion of your attention or brain power and you are less effective and less efficient.

To avoid this reduction in proficiency you must focus only on one thing at a time – keep your sole task at the forefront of your attention and don't let distractions (including music, TV, messaging, etc.) get in the way.

## The Film is Just as Good as the Book

Having taught English for many years I have heard this one a lot. Many students have watched the film instead of reading the book, thinking that they can take a shortcut. Watching the film is much quicker than having to read the book and you can usually do it with a drink and popcorn. Unfortunately, there are a few problems with this idea. Firstly, the film is NEVER just like the book – to make films based on books screen writers must tear the book apart, throw most of it away and change much of what they keep. Secondly, films and books are completely different mediums – they construct and present ideas differently (images versus words) so if you know the film it doesn't mean you know the book. Thirdly, a film based upon a book is the director's interpretation of the book – when you watch a film you are seeing one person's perspective on the book – that's why some films have multiple remakes (like Romeo and Juliet). Lastly, the process of reading the book – reading the words, seeing the action and hearing the dialogue in your mind – helps you to understand and appreciate the book so much more than watching a film can, and it will help you remember it more accurately. So, watch the film, by all means – but NOT as a substitute, but as an addition – use it for context, further study and to increase your range and level of understanding of the book.

**Homework is a Waste of Time**

The conflict over homework is a global one. Around the world groups of academics, parents and teachers argue for or against the benefits or dangers of homework. Stuck in the middle of this fight are you, the students. There are many arguments on both sides of the issue but both sides fail to understand exactly what homework can be. So, is homework a waste of time?

If homework is given just for the sake of giving homework, then yes, it can be a waste of time. If it is given **without** a clear understanding of the types of homework and how they all fit into an effective study program then homework will mostly be a waste of time. If homework is given without the expectation of being checked and corrected later then it is useless and should probably not be done.

However, if you understand the importance of homework as defined in this book (see Part 7: Homework) and you plan your work at home with clear goals in mind then your evenings will be productive and you will be successful. Homework is usually given to students to ensure that they complete their work but if you are motivated and take charge of your own learning then homework is under your control and can make your evenings extremely productive.

## Work Harder

You may think it strange that this appears in the section on myths, but as the saying goes 'you should work smarter, not harder'. This means that it's not how much time you put into your study but how effective your use of that time is. For example, if Student 'A' spends six hours studying, but during that time he is listening to music, messaging his friends and has no clear goals his time is not used effectively. Conversely, if Student 'B' works for only two hours but has clear goals, plans her time wisely and eliminates all distractions her time will be used much more effectively. Even though, on the surface, it seems that Student 'A' is working harder than Student 'B' the quality of work produced by Student 'B' would be much higher.

It's important to focus on 'quality' not 'quantity' when thinking about study. 30 minutes spent focusing on one task is better than 90 minutes when you are thinking about one task amongst many, are surrounded by distractions and have no clear goals. Working 'smarter' doesn't mean looking for the quick way to complete tasks, rather it's working out what is the best way – sometimes that may take longer, but most times a planned, organised approach will be quicker and better. Think about your time as a precious resource (like money) you shouldn't just throw it around and spend it unwisely – invest it, use it wisely and make every second count.

## Reading is Only for Those Who Want to be Writers or English Teachers

"I don't need to read because I'm going to be a scientist." "Reading is not important to me because I'm going into computing." "I'm not a reader – mathematics is my specialty." I've heard these statements and many others just like them from students who didn't feel that reading was important for them, but there are a few problems with the idea behind these statements. Firstly, regardless of which career a student plans to enter when they finish school, they must first finish school – and for that, reading is a requirement. Secondly, there are very few professional jobs in which reading is not necessary. If you wish to work in a factory, drive a bus, sweep streets or dig holes then you probably won't need to read much but for everything else reading will be a part of the job.

If you want to be a scientist you will need to keep up to date in your field – that will require reading scientific journals and reports. If you want to go onto computing you will still be required to read technical journals and reviews. If you want to be successful in any field which requires further study you will need to read – and the higher you go, the more you will need to read. Does that mean that you cannot advance in your chosen field without reading? Not necessarily, but it does mean that you will not be successful, or as successful as you can be, without reading. In today's society, without reading you cannot learn and without learning you cannot improve. Reading equals learning and the more of it you do the better you will become.

**I'll get Better Results with a Computer**
Earlier we spoke about many of the benefits and dangers of technology. Like any tool, it can be used effectively, or it can get in the way of your success. One popular myth, which seems to be common amongst parents, is the idea that students will perform better if they have a computer. I've heard this many times and have had to gently reinforce the idea that computers are just 'tools', not magic bullets.

As I've said before, I have seen many students without computers who have done very well in high school and many more students with computers who have not. A computer can be as much of a distraction as it can be an advantage – it all depends on how it is used. Someone who is organised and has self-discipline will be able to use their computer in the ways that is best going to serve them, but someone who is not organised and has no self-discipline will find their time being wasted on social media, music, messaging and an endless supply of distracting apps and activities.

In addition to this, there are many activities which cannot be completed successfully with a computer. Practical tasks including painting, drawing and modelling require a hands-on approach and as we've already discussed, taking effective notes is best done on paper. In addition, computers cannot do your thinking for you. So just like a pair of shoes doesn't make you a good runner, a computer will not make you a good student, of course a pair of shoes can make a good runner better and in the same way a computer can make a good student better. Your task is to be the good student.

## Lots of People Survive on Three Hours Sleep
This myth is usually spread by those people who want to excuse their own bad habits. The truth is very clear: science has demonstrated the benefits of sleep and the

requirements of **at least** eight hours (usually more) sleep for school-aged children – that's you! Numerous studies have been conducted on this topic and all of them reach the same conclusion – lack of sleep causes the brain to be less effective, not more. In fact, even mild sleep deprivation has been likened to being drunk (reduced reaction time, thinking ability and judgement).

Also, the urban myth that geniuses of the past (such as Albert Einstein) have achieved great things on less sleep than 'normal' people is false. In fact, sources point to the fact the Einstein had around 10 hours of sleep each night, in addition to taking afternoon naps! As we age we do tend to sleep less, but we also tend to lose elasticity in our brains, so it is not something that I would recommend. Put simply, when you are young, more sleep is better.

### More Myths
If there are more myths you want discussed do not hesitate to contact me with your suggestions. Send an email to dillon@howtosucceedathighschool.com

# Resources

Each of the following resources has been added for you to use if you wish. Read the relevant section of the book for information on how to use the resource and feel free to change the resource to suit your own ways of doing things.

Each of these templates can be easily created as a table in WORD or EXCEL (or other equivalent software). Simply add or delete columns, rows or cells and resize them as needed. The finished template can be printed out for display on walls, fridges, etc.

## Study Timetable Blank

| | Sun. | Mon. | Tues. | Wednes. | Thurs. | Fri. | Satur. |
|---|---|---|---|---|---|---|---|
| 4:00-4:30 | | | | | | | |
| 4:30-5:00 | | | | | | | |
| 5:00-5:30 | | | | | | | |
| 5:30-6:00 | | | | | | | |
| 6:00-6:30 | | | | | | | |
| 6:30-7:00 | | | | | | | |
| 7:00-7:30 | | | | | | | |
| 7:30-8:00 | | | | | | | |
| 8:00-8:30 | | | | | | | |
| 8:30-9:00 | | | | | | | |
| 9:00-9:30 | | | | | | | |
| 9:30-10:00 | | | | | | | |
| 10:00-10:30 | | | | | | | |

## Personal Timetable Blank

| | Sun. | Mon. | Tues. | Wednes. | Thurs. | Fri. | Satur. |
|---|---|---|---|---|---|---|---|
| 6:00-6:30 | | | | | | | |
| 6:30-7:00 | | | | | | | |
| 7:00-7:30 | | | | | | | |
| 7:30-8:00 | | | | | | | |
| 8:00-8:30 | | | | | | | |
| 8:30-9:00 | | | | | | | |
| 9:00-9:30 | | | | | | | |
| 9:30-10:00 | | | | | | | |
| 10:00-10:30 | | | | | | | |
| 10:30-11:00 | | | | | | | |
| 11:00-11:30 | | | | | | | |
| 11:30-12:00 | | | | | | | |
| 12:00-12:30 | | | | | | | |
| 12:30-1:00 | | | | | | | |
| 1:00-1:30 | | | | | | | |
| 1:30-2:00 | | | | | | | |
| 2:00-2:30 | | | | | | | |
| 2:30-3:00 | | | | | | | |
| 3:00-3:30 | | | | | | | |
| 3:30-4:00 | | | | | | | |
| 4:00-4:30 | | | | | | | |
| 4:30-5:00 | | | | | | | |
| 5:00-5:30 | | | | | | | |
| 5:30-6:00 | | | | | | | |
| 6:00-6:30 | | | | | | | |
| 6:30-7:00 | | | | | | | |
| 7:00-7:30 | | | | | | | |
| 7:30-8:00 | | | | | | | |
| 8:00-8:30 | | | | | | | |
| 8:30-9:00 | | | | | | | |
| 9:00-9:30 | | | | | | | |
| 9:30-10:00 | | | | | | | |
| 10:00-10:30 | | | | | | | |
| 10:30-11:00 | | | | | | | |

# Hamburger Method Template

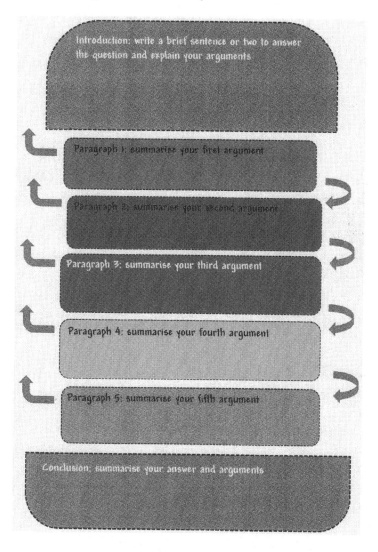

## Progress Review Template

| Progress Check for Day / Week / Term / Year |
| --- |
| What went well? |
| What didn't go well? |
| In what areas can I improve? |
| What actions can I take to improve? |